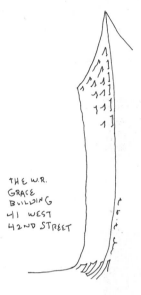

THE W.R.
GRACE
BUILDING
41 WEST
42ND STREET

NEW YORK'S 50 BEST

SKYSCRAPERS

ERIC NASH

**DRAWINGS BY
ROBERT MILES PARKER**

CITY & COMPANY
New York

New York's 50 Best Cover Concept
Copyright © 1995 by Nancy Steiny
Cover and text of Skyscrapers
Copyright © 1997 by Heather Zschock
Drawings copyright © 1997 by Robert Miles Parker
Creative Coordinator: Kristin Frederickson

Library of Congress Cataloging-in-Publication Data
Nash, Eric Peter.
New York's 50 best skyscrapers / Eric Nash.
p. cm.
ISBN 1-885492-47-2
1. Skyscrapers—New York (State)—New York—Guidebooks. 2. New York
(N.Y.)—Buildings, structures, etc.—Guidebooks. I. Title.
NA6232.N38   1997
720' .483—dc21
First Edition
Printed in the United States of America

City & Company
22 West 23rd Street
New York, NY 10010

PER ELENA

TABLE OF CONTENTS

Listings in chronological order

INTRODUCTION

Everyone has a favorite New York skyscraper, and deciding which one is best can spark a lively argument. Do you like the clean, Modernist lines of the Empire State Building, the Chrysler's rococo spire, or the classically inspired Flatiron Building? Whatever your preference, New York City has the greatest variety of skyscrapers in the world to choose from.

The skyscraper is as American an invention as jazz, Western movies, and Cadillac fins. The first generation of skyscrapers was built in Chicago after the Great Fire of 1871. Skyscrapers were in great demand, because their coated steel structures were fire resistant, and because their new height greatly multiplied the value of a piece of property. In 1900, Cass Gilbert, the architect of Manhattan's Woolworth Building, defined the skyscraper as "a machine that makes the land pay."

The origin of the word skyscraper is cloudy. It originally referred to a tall horse, or to the topmost sail of a ship, but in the late 1880s came to mean a tall building (at the time, that was anything over ten stories, which was close to the limits of how tall a stone building could be). Other contemporaneous terms such as cloudscraper fell into disuse. Loosely speaking, a skyscraper means any very tall building for its time. There are some technical considerations, chiefly that the walls are supported by a connecting frame of cast iron and/or steel.

The buildings in this book are arranged chronologically, so that you can trace the evolution of the skyscraper form, from the early eclectic styles, through the classic Art Deco silhouette, up to the International Style "glass box" and contemporary Postmodern designs. (By the way, don't be intimidated by architectural terms—they are just a shorthand for some basic concepts. A glossary is provided on page 116.)

Some of the country's, and the world's, best-known architects are well represented by New York's skyscrapers, including Louis Sullivan, Raymond Hood, Philip Johnson, Mies van der Rohe, Le Corbusier and Eero Saarinen. A great architect's individual style is as recognizable as a Picasso. As you get to know these buildings, you will come to look on them as old (and tall) friends.

In most cities around the country, it would be difficult to find fifty tall buildings; in New York, the preponderance of skyscrapers necessitated limiting the list to just fifty entries of what I consider the best. Add your own favorites to this list as you go along. And don't forget to take your binoculars—the greatest open–air skyscraper museum in the world is right outside your door.

BAYARD-CONDICT BUILDING

65–69 Bleecker Street bet. Broadway and Lafayette Street
1898, Louis H. Sullivan

A s you walk uptown on Crosby Street in SoHo, the slender, cream-colored terra-cotta façade of the Bayard-Condict Building peers out like a Cinderella among its sooty neighbors. The architect, Louis Henry Sullivan of Chicago, was the first master of skyscraper design, and this delicate tower is his only building in New York.

Sullivan's breakthrough was to make a tall building *look* tall, rather than disguise its height with designs taken from the past. The skyscraper was something new on the face of the earth, and Sullivan wrote that it "must be tall, every inch of it tall . . .that from bottom to top it is a unit without a single dissenting line."

Sullivan pioneered the concept of verticality—that the design of a building should create a sense of height in the eye of the beholder. At 13 stories, the Bayard-Condict is not significantly taller than its clunky, neoclassical neighbors, but it appears to float above them. Everything about the design contributes to the visual sense of sweep. The piers (long, vertical elements in the façade) run without interruption from the second floor to the arches at the top, so that the whole building is perceived as a unity. The floor-to-ceiling heights also diminish as you look up, from 15 feet on the ground floor to 9 1/2 feet at the twelfth story, which enhances the sense of height. The top floor enlarges to 14 1/2 feet, and combines visually on the façade with the floor below to create the effect of a capital on a column.

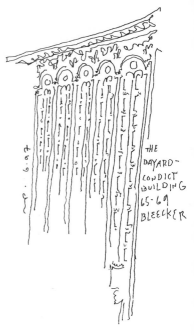

THE BAYARD-CONDICT BUILDING 65-69 BLEECKER

Sullivan, who was Frank Lloyd Wright's mentor, was known for saying "form ever follows function." The Bayard-Condict Building tells us how it is constructed: the weight-bearing steel columns that frame and support the building are expressed with broad piers, alternating with thin, purely decorative colonettes.

Named for its original owners, William Bayard, of a prominent Dutch Colonial family (Bayard Street is also named for them), and Silas Condict, a businessman—the building combines decorative elements taken from Art Nouveau, Celtic art, and the English Arts and Crafts movement. The six exquisite terra-cotta Winged Victories that crown the structural piers seem to soar above the city.

PARK ROW BUILDING

15 Park Row bet. Ann and Beekman Streets
1899, R. H. Robertson

T he Park Row Building is more important for historical reasons than strictly aesthetic ones. At the beginning of the twentieth-century, the 30-story, 391-foot-tall building, with its twin cupolas, was the tallest in the world. It is a fascinating example of the evolving skyscraper form. With its combination of nostalgia and far-sightedness, the Park Row Building epitomizes the eclectic skyscraper of the period.

The building occupies an irregularly shaped plot formed by the intersection of Ann Street and Theater Alley, but its entire appearance is oriented toward the commercially valuable Park Row front, facing City Hall. The plain red brick of the side walls contrasts sharply with the sculpted limestone and buff brick façade. The building also does not seem to have a distinct profile: wings jut out at odd angles like the arms of a starfish. It seems that architect R. H. Robertson did not have a clear understanding of the tall building as a free-standing form.

The four colossal caryatids that take up the entire fourth floor are another interesting discontinuity between the form and structure of the building. Caryatids are Classical motifs that suggest the supporting power of stone. Yet this is a building held together by steel, as plainly seen in the bare girders that span the light court on the east side. The limestone figures were carved by the sculptor John Massey Rhind, who also sculpted the allegorical figures of Victory and Peace above the entrance to Grant's Tomb.

The four-story tall, copper-roofed cupolas exemplify the essentially romantic view of technology that prevailed at the turn of the century. Machines were not yet glorified, as they were in the 1920s, and the public preferred to view technological achievements, such as the world's tallest building, through a sentimental haze of the past. The cupolas originally were open as public observation spaces, and sightseers could take in the views of Manhattan island while strolling under neoclassical domes.

The building is amazingly well-preserved. Except for the J&R World signs outside, the two-story bronze and sculpted granite base is unchanged. The lobby is a real treat. The walls are lined in rich, red-veined marble, and gilded rosettes adorn the coffered ceiling. The pièce de résistance is the original, semicircular elevator cabs that fan out like the sections of a cross-cut orange.

FLATIRON BUILDING

175 Fifth Avenue bet. East 22nd and East 23rd Streets
1902, Daniel H. Burnham

The prow-shaped Flatiron Building, one of the most prominently sited free-standing skyscrapers in New York, has captured the public's imagination ever since it was built in 1902. The design of the 21-story tower, which tapers to a gravity-defying six-foot-wide apex, was so revolutionary that turn-of-the-century New Yorkers made bets on whether the rubble would reach as far as Madison Avenue when the tower toppled over in the first high wind. Originally named the Fuller Building for its developer, it was quickly nicknamed the Flatiron Building because of its shape.

The secret of the Flatiron is that it is not a traditional masonry building, supported by heavy stone walls, but rather something new: a fully steel-framed skyscraper, much closer in spirit and construction to the later Empire State

Building. With its richly modeled limestone and terra-cotta façade, here is a building very much in the Classical vein, yet in a shape never seen in antiquity.

The building's architect, Daniel Burnham, expressed the proud spirit of the Flatiron when he said, "Make no little plans, they have no magic to stir men's blood." The Flatiron's magic is that your experience of it changes depending upon how you approach it. From the side, the Flatiron resembles a broad palazzo, but as you near the apex at 23rd Street, the perspective shifts dizzily so that the building looks like a wall only six feet thick. Bay windows eight stories tall give the sense that the façade is undulating, like a terra-cotta curtain, adding a Modern dynamism to neoclassical repose.

The whole building seems to be in motion, restlessly impelling the observer to view it from different angles. The photographer Alfred Stieglitz observed that it "appeared to be moving toward me like the bow of a monster ocean steamer—a picture of new America still in the making."

"LITTLE SINGER" BUILDING

561 Broadway bet. Prince and Spring Streets
1904, Ernest Flagg

This 12-story former factory for the Singer Sewing Machine Company, with its green-painted metal, recessed glass, and textured red terra-cotta façade, is a gem of a building of a type little seen in New York: a Parisian-style commercial building from the turn of the century. Almost every major American architect of the time studied at the Ecole des Beaux-Arts in Paris, yet few designed buildings in the contemporary French style.

Ernest Flagg, who also designed the elegant Parisian-influenced Scribner's Building on Fifth Avenue, believed that new building materials such as cast iron and glass should be used in a way that would express the underlying construction of a building. Skyscrapers, after all, were not supported by thick stone walls, like medieval forts, but rather were self-supporting steel cages covered with a thin skin of glass or masonry.

Flagg's "Little Singer" acquired the nickname to distinguish it from his 47-story Singer Tower at Broadway and Liberty Street, which was the tallest building in the world when it was built in 1908, and now has the dubious distinction of being the tallest building ever to be demolished.

The "Little Singer" is beautifully ornamented in the style of the late nineteenth century, but at the same time it presents a breathtakingly Modern front. The façade appears to be a sheer wall of glass, anticipating by decades the look of a present-day office building.

The building boldly announces the twentieth-century aesthetic of the machine. Plain rivets declare its underlying steel construction, and the repeating patterns of metal spandrels celebrate the beauty of the machine age. But the "Little Singer" is also a craftsman's version of modernity: the intricate iron balconies are hand-wrought. Tour the interior of the ground floor, now Kate's Paperie, to get a feel of the building's airy, open construction.

WEST STREET BUILDING

90 West Street bet. Albany and Cedar Streets
1907, Cass Gilbert

I n this splendid example of early, eclectic skyscraper design, you can see the Modern form of the skyscraper come into being. Cass Gilbert's 23-story office tower anticipates the rich Gothic terra-cotta decoration of his better known Woolworth Building (page 22).

While the ornamentation of the West Street Building is Gothic, the overall design is Modern in that it expresses how the building is constructed. The shaft-like midsection, clad in white terra-cotta panels above a plain granite base, is organized much like Sullivan's Bayard-Condict Building (page 10), so that we can see what is structural and what is decorative. Broad, fluted piers that cover the structural steel columns alternate with thin, decorative three-quarter-round columns topped with Corinthian capitals.

There is a wonderful, sculptural progression base to top, as the decoration becomes more and more elaborate. The deeply recessed rounded arches of the crown, ornamented with a luxurious explosion of green and white terra-cotta rosettes, are a startling contrast to the relatively plain base. The mansarded and dormered copper roof is an early example of American corporations' use of architecture for symbolic display, a process that culminated in the Chrysler Building (page 50). The abstract, mansarded crown of Cesar Pelli's One World Financial Center (page 104), across the street, is a Postmodern tribute to the West Street Building and its gilded age.

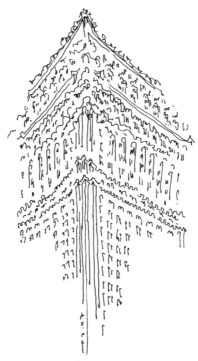

WEST STREET BUILDING
90 WEST STREET BETWEEN
ALBANY AND CEDAR

METROPOLITAN LIFE TOWER

One Madison Avenue at 24th Street
1909, Napoleon LeBrun

This Venetian-style clock tower blends inconspicuously into Madison Square Park's skyline, but at a height of 700 feet, it was once the tallest building in the world, until it was capped by the Woolworth Building (page 22) in 1913. Copied from the Campanile in Venice's Piazza San Marco, the tower does not look as high as it really is because Classical proportions lose their effect on such a big scale.

In a kind of optical illusion, the eye shrinks the building back down to size. This campanile is more than twice as tall as its counterpart in Venice, yet the mind insists on fitting the tower into the smaller scale of the original. From across the park, it just looks like a comfortably sized midrange tower. Not that this is all bad—it's just that monuments should look, well, more monumental.

The details of the tower fight a proper sense of scale. Its four clocks are huge—the numerals alone are 4 feet high on faces 26$\frac{1}{2}$-feet in diameter, and the minute hands weigh half a ton each—but their great distance from the ground makes them appear much smaller. Compare the Met Life Tower with the Flatiron Building (page 14) across the park, which at less than half the height has a greater sense of verticality and is thoroughly Modern.

The steel-framed tower was renovated with a limestone skin in the early 1960s, and much of the original white marble covering was destroyed. Step into the 320 Park Avenue entrance of this block-through building, and have a look at the 14$\frac{1}{2}$ foot long architect's drawing of the Met Life Tower, done on a scale of $\frac{1}{4}$-inch to one foot. You'll see that the tower once boasted such architectural details as wreaths, lions' heads, and dolphin balustrades, now long gone.

WOOLWORTH BUILDING

233 Broadway bet. Park Place and Barclay Street
1913, Cass Gilbert

When the architect Cass Gilbert received the Woolworth commission, there was no strong precedent for what a 767-foot-tall building (which on completion would be the tallest in the world) should look like. Gilbert came up with an ingenious solution that in retrospect seems simple: he stacked a thirty-story tower on top of a larger thirty-story base. In so doing, he created a forerunner of the setback look of the Art Deco skyscrapers to come.

Gilbert decorated his tower in a style appropriately called Flamboyant Gothic. The Woolworth's richly decorative piers, pinnacles, and spandrels are molded in cream-colored terra cotta, becoming more colorful toward the top, with highlights of green, gold, deep rose, and cobalt blue. Gothic detailing, which added to the sense of verticality in medieval cathedrals, gives the skyscraper a unified style. At the same time, the light material of the cladding emphasizes the very Modern idea that the walls of a building are not supports, but only a decorative skin.

The Woolworth abounds in marvelous contradictions. Lobby gargoyles represent the company founder Frank Woolworth counting out his coins and Cass Gilbert holding a scale replica of the building itself. The elevators, once run by smartly uniformed operators and seen as the acme of high tech, are crowned with medieval pointed arches.

The ceilings on each floor are twelve feet high, a feature that would be desirable but extravagant even for a residential building. (Today, an additional twenty stories would be packed into a building of the same height.) The building is also unusual in that it had no mortgage, or debt of any kind, as Frank Woolworth, the five-and-dime king, paid the $13-million-dollar construction costs in cash.

THE WOOLWORTH
BUILDING
233 BROADWAY

CANDLER BUILDING

220 W. West 42nd Street bet. Seventh and Eighth Avenues
1914, Willauer, Shape & Bready

The beauty of this 24-story building is its simplicity rather than its ornateness. Originally the New York headquarters of the Coca-Cola Company, and named for its founder, Asa Candler, the building represents a turning point between the elaborately decorated, eclectic-style skyscraper and the emerging, simple silhouette of the Modernist skyscraper.

The Candler Building makes an interesting comparison with Cass Gilbert's 90 West Street (page 18). Both buildings are faced in terra cotta, and both were inspired by historical styles, Spanish Renaissance for the Candler and neo-Gothic for 90 West Street. The Candler Building, however, recently restored and gleaming white, is a greatly simplified version of revival architecture, the result of economic considerations. Workman-ship was becoming more expensive in the second decade of the twentieth century, so architects were making a virtue out of necessity by developing a new, cleaner style.

The Candler is significant because it was one of the earliest buildings to use setbacks—the steplike indentations that form the silhouette of an archetypal Art Deco skyscraper. The features are just in embryo here—the base is made up of little more than vestigial "wings" (one of them now missing), and the crown steps back only a few feet from the shaft—yet the plan served as a model for two other important 42nd Street skyscrapers, Bush Tower (page 26) and the American Radiator Building (page 30).

Later skyscrapers would continue to follow this model of a wide, impressive base, a rather plain shaft with a regular, repeating pattern for many floors, and a setback symbolic crown. The Candler's windows, especially those on the east and west elevations completely devoid of decorative frames, set a pattern that would be repeated in many Deco skyscrapers including the Empire State Building (page 52). The large, round-headed windows that mark the crown create the visual effect of a column topped off with a capital. The pattern is much like Cass Gilbert's design for the West Street Building, but here the arches are simplified.

Decorative flourishes were saved for the crown. Without binoculars (which are highly recommended for all the buildings in this book), it's hard to see that the Candler's crown is graced with giant terra-cotta sea horses, delicate tracery, and faces of women. One might ask why such fine detail was placed so far from the street, but I think it was a matter of corporate pride. Businessmen were showing off their accomplishments to other denizens of the high realm. Thus, the skyscraper can be seen as a kind of twentieth-century totem pole, with the most important images in the highest places.

BUSH TOWER

130–132 West 42nd Street
bet. Avenue of the Americas and Broadway
1918, Harvey Wiley Corbett

Four limestone gargoyles at the base of Bush Tower hint at its original use as headquarters for the Bush Terminal Company, whose vast shipping, storage, and manufacturing businesses once occupied 150 buildings and 8 piers sprawled over nearly 30 blocks of the West Side. The gargoyles represent a navigator with his sextant; a hardy helmsman wearing a sou'wester; a frightened cabin boy clutching a mast; and a sailor wrapping himself around an anchor.

Architect Harvey Wiley Corbett was primarily interested in the power of the Gothic style to suggest vertical thrust, rather than in faithfully copying a historical style. Corbett, one of the visionaries who helped dream up the Manhattan of the 1920s, sensed that it was not modern simply to stretch Gothic ornament onto tall buildings. Instead, his gray limestone Bush Tower presents merely a suggestion, or representation, of Gothic style. The skinny vertical bays typical of English Gothic are neatly adapted to the tower's dramatically narrow front, 480 feet tall but only 50 feet wide. Gothic detailing is reserved for the giant copper pinnacles at the first setback, and for the filigreed crown. Flat, trompe l'oeil piers in colored brick simulate the light and shadow cast by Gothic design.

Bush Tower was New York's last major tall building to be designed before the 1916 zoning code, which required that the upper levels of buildings be set back by a designated number of feet from the street, changing the playing field forever. Corbett used a setback here mainly to disguise the water tank and elevator housing, but the building's *parti* would become the prototype for the great Deco towers to follow.

THE BUSH
BUILDING
42ND STREET
BETWEEN
6TH AND 7TH

SHELTON TOWERS HOTEL

(now Marriott East Side Hotel)

525 Lexington Avenue bet. East 48th and East 49th Streets
1924, Arthur Loomis Harmon

When painter Georgia O'Keeffe and her husband, photographer Alfred Stieglitz, moved into a tiny, two-bedroom apartment on the Shelton's twenty-eighth floor, they helped turn the skyscraper into an icon of American modern art. From the windows of the Shelton, Stieglitz photographed the crackling crown of the old RCA Victor Building (page 62) and the German Expressionist copper turrets of the Waldorf-Astoria (page 58). O'Keeffe painted the Shelton in varying lights, the way Monet painted Chartres, but she used effects borrowed from photography to create her paintings *Shelton Hotel, New York, No. 1* and *The Shelton with Sunspots*.

Designed by Arthur Loomis Harmon in the Lombardy Revival style, the Shelton was the first building to make use of the aesthetic possibilities afforded by the 1916 setback zoning code. Harmon treated the massive surface of warm yellow brick as a sculpted solid, making the setbacks an integral part of the building's visual sweep, rather than an applied afterthought.

Classical masonry techniques give the building a Modernist

unity. The limestone base is battered, meaning it slants inward, to counteract the feeling of a building looming over the pedestrians below. The top setback employs entasis, the Classical Greek method of giving a slight bulge to vertical elements such as a column, to counteract the illusion of concavity produced by a long vertical line. Patterns of raised brick add shadow and texture to the surface.

Look closely at the delightfully kitschy carved limestone panels above the entrance. The Shelton originally opened as an apartment hotel and sports club for men, which accounts for the carved figures of a swimmer toweling off and a player in a toga with a racquet and two tennis balls. The basement pool with lion's head spouts, where Houdini once performed an escape, is now closed.

AMERICAN RADIATOR BUILDING

**40 West 40th Street bet. Fifth and Sixth Avenues
1924, Raymond Hood**

Black office buildings are now commonplace, but the American Radiator Building, named for the heating company that owned it, was the first one in New York. Raymond Hood's glazed brick office building towered like a dark Gothic knight over the Beaux-Arts public library at its foot, a challenge to the chaste, white, and horizontally oriented styles of the past.

Hood, who studied with the Gothic revivalist architect Ralph Adams Cram, was more interested in what Gothic detailing could do to heighten a building's sense of verticality than he was in faithfully duplicating a historical style. The Radiator presents two façades in one: a Modernist, unaccented shaft with an abrupt shift to the Gothic-style, gilded terra-cotta pinnacles of the crown. The complex rhythm of square and round-headed windows in the crown recall Cass Gilbert's West Street Building (page 18).

A few small touches give the Radiator a powerful feeling of height, although it is just 22 stories tall. The corners of the shaft are chamfered, so that the tower appears to be one sculptural surface. The tower is also set in slightly from the walls of neighboring buildings, so that it is seen as standing alone. Unfortunately, the luxurious lobby has been closed to the public for years because the building is untenanted.

The Radiator's gilded pinnacles originally were lit up dramatically at night. Hood took the mission of the American Radiator Company quite literally, and intended the crown to resemble a "pile of coal, glowing at the top." Georgia O'Keeffe was so struck with the building's image that she painted *Radiator Building—Night, New York.* She couldn't resist taking a sly poke at its advertising function and painted in her husband's name, Alfred Stieglitz, as a red neon sign against the skyline.

PARAMOUNT BUILDING

1501 Broadway bet. West 43rd and West 44th Streets
1926, C. W. Rapp & George L. Rapp

The 29-story Paramount Building personifies Broadway razzle-dazzle. Its cascading pyramidal setbacks and spectacular, two-story-tall four-sided clock were built to show off the power and prestige of its owner, Paramount Pictures. Through these doors walked such Paramount stars as Mae West, Gloria Swanson, and Gary Cooper.

The nineteen-foot-in-diameter glass globe on top (once illuminated from within) signifies Paramount's interests around the world, while glowing, five-pointed stars, a Paramount trademark, denote the hours on the clockfaces. The building's eight buff brick setbacks were once lit up at night to enhance their dramatic, Modernist effect, a quite literal interpretation of the 1916 zoning cade. It's no surprise that the Chicago firm of Rapp & Rapp was known throughout the country for their lavish movie palaces.

Old photographs of Times Square show the undulating canopy that marked the entrance to the Paramount Theater, which was once housed within the building near the 43rd Street side. It was here that bobby-soxers swooned to Frank Sinatra in the 1940s, and Buddy Holly headlined Alan Freed's Christmas rock 'n' roll review in 1957. Sadly, the opulent 3,650-seat theater, ten stories high and with three balconies, was gutted and converted into office space in 1964. Even the grand, arched entry has been reconstructed (you can tell where it once stood by the sealed-over windows just below the top of the base). The clocks no longer run, making the pyramidal Paramount look even more like a remnant from some lost civilization, although a major renovation is under way.

Like many buildings of the period, the Paramount exhibits a bit of a split personality: its exterior is pure Deco, while the lobby is studiously Neoclassical. Masks of Comedy and Tragedy are emblazoned on the bronze panels above the revolving door, and Classical figures of women playing harps and bagpipes top the gorgeously worked bronze elevator doors.

THE
PARAMOUNT
BUILDING
1501 BROADWAY

BARCLAY-VESEY BUILDING

140 West Street bet. Barclay and Vesey Streets
1926, Ralph Walker

The Barclay-Vesey Building, originally built to house switching equipment as well as 6,000 employees of the New York Telephone Company, marked a radical departure from historical styles of architecture. Nothing quite like this had ever been seen before.

The 32-story building, which looks like a mountain of warm, brown brick capped in white stone, relies on the arrangement of its mass-

BARCLAY-
VESEY
BUILDING
ON WEST
STREET

ing rather than on decoration for its effect. The base and tower change in relation to each other as the viewer changes position. From some vantage points, the acute angles make the walls seem paper thin, while from the obtuse corners the building appears massive and slablike. There is a constant dialogue and interplay between the two aspects. Rather than being in Classical repose,

Modern buildings such as this one offer a kind of instability, which requires the viewer to complete the picture.

Although the lobby guards can be a little testy, step inside for a look at the spectacular, marble-lined space, one of the best Deco interiors in the city. The elaborate murals and bronze floor plaques are a tribute to the world of communications. The Barclay-Vesey was the first building in the Modernist style to receive an award from the prestigious Architectural League. Ralph Walker's colleague Raymond Hood crowed: "The Modernist has always been the underdog, but when a distinctly Modern structure like the new telephone building wins the League's gold medal of honor, his position and that of the Classicist have been reversed."

New York now belonged to the Modernists.

FRED F. FRENCH BUILDING

551 Fifth Avenue at 45th Street
1927, Fred F. French Co., H. Douglas Ives,
and Sloan & Robertson

A twentieth century office tower built in the shape of a Babylonian ziggurat is not quite as far-fetched as it first seems. Pyramids were a natural source of ideas for architects who were looking for ways to conform to the setback zoning code of 1916. Skyscraper crowns of the Art Deco period reflected Egyptian, Mayan, and Aztec influences. The French Building's complicated series of small setbacks resembles an entire village of Babylonian ziggurats.

The French Building looked to Assyrian art, with its brightly painted polychrome bas-reliefs, as a rich source of color. Four brilliantly hued glazed tile panels decorate the crown, and the vibrant orange brick setbacks are trimmed in red, black, green, and gold tile. (By the way, the 38-story building was one of the first skyscrapers in the world with a flat roof, a radical departure at the time.)

The face of Mercury, the god of commerce, is depicted as a rising sun on the brilliant east and west elevations that face the sunrise and sunset. The grand panels to the north and south show, according

unity of this building with some of the earliest eclectic experiments such as the Park Row Building (p.12).

The play of light over the surface is marvelously sculptural. The direct rays of sunrise over the East River add depth and texture to the starkly undecorated setbacks, while the more mellow light of sunset makes the orange walls softly glow in the shadows. The walls between the piers taper in at the cornices, deepening the shadows. Round, open arches at the top echo the Art Deco frozen-fountain motifs in cast stone at the base.

The building originally was a residential hotel for women who belonged to a group of sororities known as the Pan-Hellenic Club. Look for the Greek letters embedded in concrete blocks on the façade of the first floor.

The Beekman still operates as a hotel, although much of the original interior no longer exists. The Top of the Tower bar features romantic views of the East River and the United Nations.

ONE FIFTH AVENUE

at East 8th Street
1929, Harvey Wiley Corbett

O ne Fifth Avenue's romantic stepped-back silhouette marks the beginning of New Yorkers' love affair with Art Deco and skyscraper living—think of William Powell in *The Thin Man*, aluminum cocktail shakers, the brittle patter of the Algonquin Round Table, and the Cole Porter lyrics "Down in the depths on the 90th floor."

As with his earlier Bush Tower (page 26), architect Harvey Wiley Corbett applied historical ornamentation to an uncompromisingly Modernist design. The distribution of limestone masses gives One Fifth the kind of distinctive, dramatically stepped-back silhouette that became the hallmark of Jazz Age architecture.

The decoration becomes progressively more schematic from base to top of the 27-story building. The base features large bronze Renaissance-style lanterns and carved stone balconies, but the piers are merely sketched in with trompe l'oeil white and black "shadow" brick. The piers end in wonderful two-dimensional pinnacles, as if to say that Modern residences need only a suggestion of historical references.

The lobby reflects the split personality of the 1920s. Well-to-do Fifth Avenue residents wanted something to show for their money, so the lobby is a double-height oak-paneled gallery in the Doric style, but a built-in wall clock sports a sleek Deco face, without numerals.

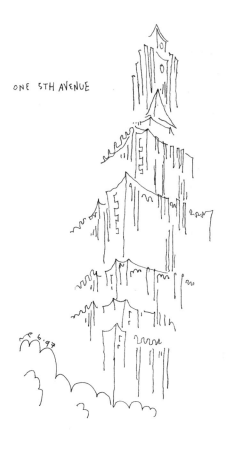

ONE 5TH AVENUE

CHANIN BUILDING

122 East 42nd Street at Lexington Avenue
1929, Sloan & Robertson

Although overshadowed by its taller and glitzier neighbor, the Chrysler Building (page 50), the 56-story Chanin Building is a wonderful combination of skyscraper styles, from Art Deco, neo-Gothic, and German Expressionism to International Style.

Irwin Chanin, a builder and Broadway producer, conceived of his headquarters in grandly theatrical terms. A promotional brochure

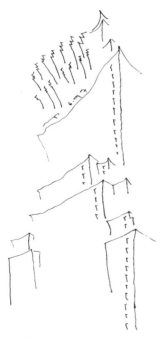

referred to the Chanin Building as the "mise en scene for the romantic drama of American business."

The Gothic buttresses of the crown, which resemble those of Saint Patrick's Cathedral, are dramatically illuminated at night, as they were originally. The lighting scheme is the opposite of daylight: shadowy recesses in the crown are lit up, making the buttresses appear as dark bars against an inner glow.

Night is cast as something romantic and distinct from day, reflecting Chanin's interest in the evening fantasy world of the theater. The fiftieth floor once contained a complete, 200-seat theater designed by the sculptor Jacques Delamarre, who also designed the wonderful, allegorical bronze lobby panels.

THE CHANIN BUILDING
122 E. 42ND STREET

Another major style evolves in the Chanin: the slab form typical of the post-war Internationalist school of architecture. The Chanin is, in fact, a proto-slab, having the appearance of a narrow tower when seen from the north or south, but resolving itself into a broad slab when viewed from other angles. Extremely shallow setbacks add to the powerful flatness of the form. The building's basic form would appear again in Raymond Hood's McGraw-Hill and RCA buildings (pages 60 and 62).

A one-story-tall, buff terra-cotta frieze of Deco-style plant forms takes up the entire third-floor façade. At street level, buttery bronze panels present a stylized vision of evolution, from marine life to flying birds. Similarly, the Chanin presents itself as the pinnacle of evolution, evidenced in the lobby's winged directory, elevator doors boasting cast bronze birds and Delamarre's bronze panels depicting man rising by thought and action to the heights.

HELMSLEY BUILDING

230 Park Avenue bet. East 45th and East 46th Streets
1929, Warren & Wetmore

The ornate limestone and ochre brick Helmsley looks like a throwback to the Beaux-Arts style that was popular at the turn of the century, but it also functions as a Modern building. Warren & Wetmore, the great Beaux-Arts team that built Grand Central Terminal, designed the Helmsley Building (originally the New York Central Building) to house the offices of the powerful New York Central railroad. The architects had several complex objectives in mind: to provide a crowning touch for the Beaux-Arts terminal, to redirect the dense flow of pedestrians and automobile traffic, and to cap off Park Avenue visually.

In a Beaux-Arts building, the circulation of people through the space is controlled like a procession. The Helmsley Building is marvelously organized and accessible: automobile roadways penetrate the front, separated from busy pedestrian arcades. The grand, block-through Louis XIV–style lobby, with its brilliant chandeliers and polished marble walls, looks as if it were lifted from Versailles and made larger. The lobby serves both as an efficient corridor for thousands of office workers and as a monument to the power and prestige of the railroads.

Although the residential character of midtown Park Avenue has changed considerably since the Helmsley was built, the embracing, fourteen-story wings of the building continue the traditional cornice line that once governed the avenue. Its pyramidal roof topped with an ornamental lantern gives Park Avenue the feeling of a grand civic foyer.

Yet the 35-story Helmsley shows the Beaux-Arts style straining at its seams to cope with its radical height. In order to be seen at street level, Beaux-Arts ornamentation on skyscrapers had to be exaggerated. Even in its day, the Helmsley was criticized for the heavy colonnade below the roof line, awkwardly supported by brackets (which violates the visual sense of weight), in turn supporting nothing but another set of brackets.

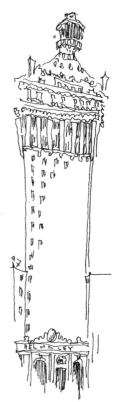

Beaux-Arts style finally succumbed to the demand for tall buildings, which made the decorative style obsolete, and to the economics of the Depression, when the materials and workmanship required for a building like the Helmsley were no longer feasible.

FULLER BUILDING

41 East 57th Street at Madison Avenue
1929, Walker & Gillette

The palette of the Fuller Building is limited to black and white, but it manages to look as dressy as a man in a tuxedo. The monochromatic tones define how the building is organized: the first six floors, framed in black granite, are filled with such lux-

ury stores as Coach, Prada, and Louis Vuitton, as well as art galleries. The white brick and smaller window openings of the shaft indicate office space. The crown is decorated with bold geometric patterns in black and white brick, punctuated by tremendous oculi, or round windows, that overlook the city in three directions.

The Fuller Company, still one of the country's largest construction firms, made its headquarters a monument to the building trade.

Although the Flatiron Building (page 14) was originally named the Fuller Building for its owners, nobody ever called it that. When the company moved uptown, it wanted to instill both its name and the image of its new 40-story skyscraper in the mind of the public. You'll see the name emblazoned over a three-story entrance flanked by Deco-style pilasters. Above the entrance, two classically styled workmen rest on their sledgehammers against a Modernist skyline in gray limestone by the sculpter Elie Nadelman.

Inside, the heavy bronze elevator doors, frequently a highlight of Deco lobbies, show construction workers on the job—laying bricks, riding a steel girder, and drilling a foundation. The lobby floor consists entirely of mosaic tile, with repeating motifs of plumb bobs and other building tools. Best of all are the large circles with blue, white, and yellow mosaics depicting highlights of the company's history. One large circle shows the new Fuller Building itself, limned in white tile with black trim, and another features the company's original headquarters, here diplomatically labeled "The Fuller Flatiron Building."

WILLIAMSBURGH SAVINGS BANK

(now Republic National Bank)

1 Hanson Place at Ashland Place, Brooklyn
1929, Halsey, McCormack & Helmer

The grand banking floor of the Williamsburgh Savings Bank is one of the city's most breathtaking interiors, with a six-story-high, vaulted gold mosaic ceiling supported by limestone columns topped with sculptural terra-cotta capitals. Just as images in a medieval church were meant as instruction for the unlettered in the ways of the Bible, the Williamsburgh Savings Bank is a shrine to the virtues of thrift.

Every detail in the bank is a lesson in the value of work and saving money. Classically styled bronze figures on the gates leading to the main floor depict the trades of Brooklyn's immigrant workers: a fruit-seller, a butcher, a bricklayer, a laborer, and a carpenter. One figure in a column capital just inside the door is even running a sewing machine.

The reasons why people should save are depicted symbolically throughout the chamber: a stork, for children and family; a beehive, to make money grow; construction workers, to represent home owner-ship; and an old man with a long beard, for retirement. At the far end of the vault, a terra-cotta lamp representing education is surrounded by terra-cotta capitals depicting a youth holding a model locomotive and a youth with a caduceus, symbolizing the engineering and the medical professions respectively. This progression of images through the bank thus represents an immigrant's dream, from the manual trades at the gates to a secure retirement and professional careers for one's children at the end.

The 512-foot, 30-story Byzantine-style office tower of buff-colored brick and terra cotta is the tallest building in Brooklyn, and it reigned as the tallest building on Long Island until the 663-foot, 48-story Citicorp office building went up in Hunters Point, Queens, in 1989. The Williamsburgh's four-sided illuminated clock under a gilded copper dome is one of the largest in the world, with clock faces that measure twenty-seven feet in diameter.

Two carved limestone panels that flank the grand, arched entry on Hanson Place are especially whimsical: the one on the right shows a cartoonish, masked burglar with a lamp and a gunnysack, the other shows a rueful convict in a padlocked cell.

CHRYSLER BUILDING

405 Lexington Avenue at 42nd Street
1930, William Van Alen

The Chrysler Building vied with the Empire State Building (page 00) and the now largely forgotten Manhattan Company Building at 40 Wall Street in a madcap, three-way dash to become the world's tallest building. The Chrysler's architect, William Van Alen, waited for his former partner turned bitter rival H. Craig Severance to cap off his neoclassically styled Manhattan Company Building at 927 feet, and then unveiled his secret weapon—the polished chrome steel spire, or "vertex" that brought the Chrysler's height to a world record 1,048 feet.

For a few shining months, the Chrysler was the tallest man-made structure in the world. Less than a year later, the Empire State would best the Chrysler, but only by two feet. The significant difference between the two buildings was actually the height of the public observation platforms—the Empire State's stood on the eighty-sixth floor, below the mast, while the Chrysler's observatory was much lower, on the sixty-ninth floor, just above the former Cloud Club.

The rippling, three-story tall black granite entrances of the Chrysler part like proscenium curtains to reveal the splendors within.

The triangular lobby lined in red Moroccan marble is one of the most extravagant to be seen in an American office building. The aesthetics here are pure Expressionist—bizarre, disorienting angles, muted onyx lighting sources, and bold Rouge Flambé patterned marble walls.

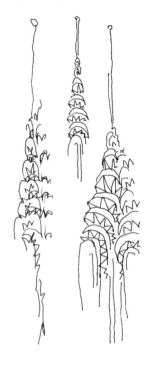

The exterior of the white brick tower might be described as Early Modern Hubcap. It's a gloriously daffy paean to the automobile. A decorative frieze of stylized hubcaps in black brick at the thirtieth floor is topped by silver "gargoyles" that recall the trademark winged radiator cap of a Chrysler automobile. Eight giant eagle heads crown the next setback. The spire might be seen as an abstraction of an eagle's feather, with the geometric plates resembling interconnecting barbules. The whole building then becomes a great eagle in flight, recalling the fantasy of motion behind the wheel of a Chrysler.

EMPIRE STATE BUILDING

350 Fifth Avenue bet. East 33rd and East 34th Streets
1931, Shreve, Lamb & Harmon

Simply put, the Empire State Building is the best known sky-scraper in the world, as immediately recognizable as the Eiffel Tower or the Taj Mahal. The 1,050-foot-tall building reigned as the world's tallest for four decades, until it was superseded by the 1,350-foot twin towers of the World Trade Center in 1973 (page 88), and by the 1,454 foot Sears Tower in Chicago a year later. Even so, it has never been replaced in the public's heart. The façade that launched a thousand souvenirs remains the quintessential icon of the Modernist spirit.

Statistics relating to the construction of the Empire State are awe-inspiring: the building required 10 million bricks, 1,172 miles of wire for the elevator cables, 6,000 windows, 2 million feet of electrical wire, and 200,000 cubic feet of stone. Of the 5,000 men who worked on the construction, 5 were killed on the job: one was hit by a truck, another died in a blast area, a third unwittingly stepped off a scaffold, a fourth fell down an elevator shaft, and a fifth was hit by a hoist. The building went up in an astonishing eighteen months.

The basic look of the building was determined by accountants rather than architects. The architect William Lamb wasn't brought on board until nearly half a year after plans were started. He tersely summed up the requirements he was given: "The program was short enough—a fixed budget, no space more than twenty-eight feet from window to corridor, as many stories of such space as possible, an exterior of limestone, and completion date of May 1, 1931."

A height of 86 floors was settled on because it would provide the optimal rate of return as well as lend the building the cachet of being the tallest in the world. The overall massing of the base and shaft reflected the zoning code and the distribution of elevators. Gray Indiana limestone was chosen for the skin because it was the most economical form of stone to assemble. Even the chrome flashing that lines the walls and gives the building a distinctive, Modernist appearance was a low-cost choice. As was typical of Deco skyscrapers, the Empire State's money was lavished on the crown, made of aluminum, nickel, and steel, and on the lobby, lined in majestic, red-veined gray marble.

The planners, however, did not count on the Great Depression, and the building was nicknamed the Empty State Building when it opened. It first turned a profit in 1950, and is now visited by more than 3.5 million people a year, almost twice as many who visit the World Trade Center.

DOWNTOWN ATHLETIC CLUB

18 West Street at Morris Street
1930, Starrett & Van Vleck

21 WEST STREET

at Morris Street
1931, Starrett & Van Vleck

These two complementary, small-scale Art Deco skyscrapers are among the best examples of the use of textured brickwork and polychromatism, or color, in buildings in New York. The intricate tilework of 21 West's façade creates a textilelike effect of warp and woof, with umber-colored piers interlacing with burnt-orange spandrels. A frieze of chevrons (which subtly complements the motif of the Athletic Club next door) is composed of raised and recessed tiles. The salt-glazed tiles that cover the 31-story office building are a visual feast, shading from dark caramel to orange, and varying richly in size and pattern. The cavernous, Moorish-style sidewalk arcade on the Morris Street side once sheltered ferry commuters.

When the Downtown Athletic Club opened in the depths of the Depression, the slender, 38-story tower of variegated burnt-orange brickwork featured a golf course on the ninth floor, complete with a flowing brooklet and real trees. The twelfth floor still contains a pool, once illuminated at night by underwater lights, so that swimmers appeared to be floating in a luminous plane over Wall Street As the Dutch architect Rem Koolhaas writes in his book, *Delirious New York:* "Nature is now resurrected *inside* the Skyscraper as merely one of its infinite layers."

The remaining floors of the club, which did not admit women until 1972, were devoted to such male pleasures as boxing, a raw oyster bar, and a barber shop with six barbers. The club still functions as an elite athletic club, open to members only. You may, however, step into the lobby for a look at the original Heisman Trophy, which is symbolically presented at the club every year to the country's best college football player.

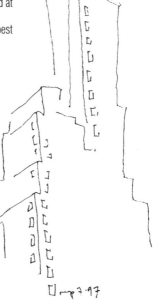

GENERAL ELECTRIC BUILDING
(originally RCA Victor Building)

570 Lexington Avenue at East 51st Street
1931, Cross & Cross

Every detail of this graceful 40-story Art Deco spire celebrates the power and prestige of the RCA Victor Corporation, which started out in radio broadcasting and record production.

To appreciate the architectural symbols, you need a sense of radio's hold on the public's imagination in the time before television. Radio was felt to be an invisible, all-powerful medium that spanned the globe. Cross & Cross, the architects of the RCA Building, represented this magical form of energy with designs of lightning bolts.

The crown of the RCA fairly crackles with electricity. Stylized radio waves interlace in open terra-cotta tracery, a brilliant fusion of Gothic and Deco styles. This charged latticework is surmounted by lightning bolts shooting heavenward, representing a broadcast signal. Gilded inlays at the top catch and reflect the rays of the sun like bolts of energy. Giant, solemn-faced figures that resemble Tiki gods look out in four directions as the embodiment of the power of radio.

The whole façade sumptuously combines a variety of materials—toothsome orange marble, salmon-hued glazed brick, gleaming metal and polychrome terra cotta—all in homage to the activities of the RCA Corporation. The terra-cotta panels just above street level, in rose, ochre and green, are a stylized version of a phonograph needle, connoting RCA's record business. At the corner of East 51 Street and Lexington Avenue, two outstretched miniature arms in metal hold crackling light-ning bolts, flanked by two fists holding raised lightning bolts, which resemble the emblem of the Strategic Air Command. The image of ener-gy worked just as well for the second owner, General Electric, who sim-ply added a clock with the GE emblem below the miniature arms. Be sure to take a look at the diamond-shaped Deco clock in the lobby, which is capped by a barrel-vaulted aluminum ceiling.

WALDORF-ASTORIA HOTEL

301 Park Avenue bet. East 49th and East 50th Streets
1931, Schultze & Weaver

The original Waldorf-Astoria, where handlebar-mustached millionaires of the Gilded Age once dined on oysters and champagne, was demolished to make way for the Empire State Building. The contract for the second hotel, a monumental city within a city on Park Avenue, was signed on October 29, 1929, the day of the stock market crash.

The gilt-lettered, 18-story limestone façade on Park Avenue conceals a labyrinth of ballrooms, restaurants, suites, and such luxe boutiques as Sulka and H. Stern. The three-story ballroom was the largest in the world when it was built; this room and the smaller ballrooms combined could accommodate 6,000 guests.

The windowless main lobby is a masterpiece of neoclassically inspired Deco design, from the figures in the grandly scaled, multicolored mosaic floor to the friezes just below ceiling level. The details are delightful, such as the intricately worked nickel entry on Park Avenue and the grace figures on the masterfully understated elevator doors. The unusually somber inner reception area is paneled in dark Oregon maple with veined black marble pilasters.

The twin, green copper domes atop the hotel's 625-foot-tall, 29-story white brick towers could have been taken directly from Fritz Lang's film *Metropolis,* which presented a vision of a future city. From East 50th Street, the towers appear to be all narrowly spaced vertical lines, giving the building a dramatic sense of height. Every U.S. president since Herbert Hoover has stayed in the towers, which provide excellent security because of their isolation. At night, with its crenellated parapets silhouetted against the spotlit, verdigris turrets, the Waldorf resembles an impregnable fortress.

THE WALDORF-
ASTORIA
PARK AVENUE
BETWEEN 49TH
AND 50TH

MCGRAW-HILL BUILDING

(former)

330 West 42nd Street bet. Eighth and Ninth Avenues
1931, Raymond Hood

When the architectural historian Henry-Russell Hitchcock and architect Philip Johnson mounted their watershed exhibit, "The International Style," at the newly started Museum of Modern Art in 1931, they included only one New York City building: the McGraw-Hill Building. As they described it, "The lightness, simplicity and lack of applied verticalism mark this skyscraper as an advance over other New York skyscrapers and bring it within the limits of the International Style."

The McGraw-Hill represents a transitional form between the setback Deco silhouette of the late 1920s and the horizontally oriented, undecorated slab form championed by Philip Johnson and other architects of the International Style. When the building is viewed directly from its uptown or downtown sides, the unaccented setbacks, in blue-green

sion between the image of the RCA as slab or tower makes the classical order around it hum with a Modernist sense of the dynamism of space. At the heart of this orderly universe, the RCA refuses to be perceived as static, so the whole space comes alive.

A complete list of the artists who collaborated on the center would exceed the limits of this book: Lee Lawrie sculpted the bronze Atlas on the Fifth Avenue side, Isamu Noguchi created the stainless steel sculpture News that appears above the entrance of the Associated Press Building on West 51st Street, and Hildreth Meier created the brilliantly colored enamel plaques that decorate the exterior of Radio City Music Hall.

The gilded statue of Prometheus by Paul Manship that floats above the skating rink originally was meant to mark a subway entrance. This was never built, and when Rockefeller Center opened, the management abruptly found themselves with an unused hole in the middle of their property. They first tried the space as a roller-skating rink, but it only served to attract young hoodlums from nearby Hell's Kitchen. Finally, someone suggested ice skating to draw a more refined crowd, and the result looks as if it was always meant to be.

CITIES SERVICE BUILDING

(now 70 Pine Street)

at Pearl Street
1932, Clinton & Russell

The Cities Service Building takes the concept of the skyscraper as a secularized cathedral to new heights. Just as stained glass windows are the glory of a Gothic cathedral, so is the colored glass crown of this 67-story tower. Not only is the top of the building illuminated at night, it actually emits light from inside, so that the crown seems to glow from within like an emerald.

The idea of colored glass architecture dates back to the writings of the German Expressionists during World War I. Nothing was built in Germany during the war, so architects created visions on paper of mystically glowing cities. In *Glass Architecture,* the theorist Paul Scheebart wrote that the effect of colored glass "corresponds to that created by windows of Gothic cathedrals . . . . Glass architecture makes homes into cathedrals."

Another way in which the Cities Service Building parallels a Gothic cathedral can be seen between its entrance doors. Just above the polished rainbow granite base, where a cathedral normally would have the figure of a saint, there is a limestone carving of the building itself.

At night, the green-hued beacon is a perfect embodiment of the romantic aspirations of the Deco era. It's hard to imagine any businessman's building such a monument today.

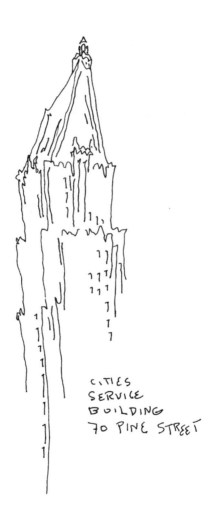

CITIES
SERVICE
BUILDING
70 PINE STREET

ONE WALL STREET
(Originally Irving Trust Building)

One Wall Street at Broadway
1932, Ralph Walker

The Irving Trust Company built its headquarters on what was at the time the most expensive plot of land in the world: One Wall Street. The lot itself, without improvements, was assessed at a whopping $30,000 per foot of frontage, or $10,250,000 in Depression dollars for this 180- by 110-foot piece of New York City. Ralph Walker designed a skyscraper worthy of the site.

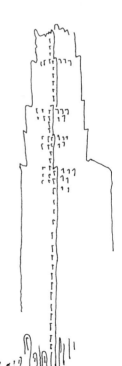

The 49-story limestone tower is that most paradoxical of things, a feminine skyscraper. Chamfered corners, a fluted limestone façade incised with featherlike motifs, and deeply recessed, faceted windows soften the starkly Modernist silhouette. The greatest treasures, however, are within. The double-height banking hall is one of the most extravagant interiors in New York. Designed by the mosaicist Hildreth Meier, the chamber looks like something out of Tsarist Russia. The walls, which ripple like the folds of a tapestry, are sheathed in gorgeous bands of deep red mosaic shading to orange and shot through with gold. A glittering bright orange and gold ceiling is lit from below by the original bronze sconces.

The observation lounge, now used as a boardroom and closed to the public, could double for the Gothic boardroom in *Batman.* From the outside, you can see the enormous, three-story-tall faceted windows on four sides of the flat-topped crown. The ceiling of the crystal-shaped chamber originally was lined with softly luminescent kapa shells. In keeping with Wall Street bankers' image of themselves, the walls were festooned with pictures of Native American war bonnets, an interesting symbol considering that this also was the site where, from 1653 to 1699, stood the six-foot-tall plank wall that protected the Dutch settlement of New Amsterdam from Indian attack, thus giving Wall Street its name.

UNITED NATIONS SECRETARIAT

United Nations Plaza, First Avenue
bet. East 42nd and East 48th Streets
1949-1952, Wallace K. Harrison, project director,
and Le Corbusier, consulting architect

The dramatic slab of the United Nations Secretariat gave New Yorkers their first look at a sheer glass wall. As if to reassure the public that such an ethereal structure could stand up on its own, the architects bracketed the glass façade between two solid bookends of sparkling white Vermont marble. From the north and south it looks more like a solid stone tower than an office building.

The slab, which measures 544 feet high, 287 feet wide, and only 72 feet deep, and features 5,400 working windows, was the tallest glass-walled building in the world when it was built. The blue-green tinted Thermopane double-glazed windows create a sense of sheerness and smoothness. Ventilation pipes are ingeniously hidden behind intake grilles at the sixth, sixteenth, and thirty-ninth floors, and the grillwork tracery of the crown disguises an old-fashioned wooden water tower. (Even the most chic modern buildings have these classic water towers on top, because wooden slats are still the only kind that do not affect the taste of the water.)

The Secretariat Building marks the ascendancy of the International Style after World War II. It symbolized the postwar world: bright, new, clean, efficient. The unadorned façade makes an interesting comparison with the romantic aspirations of the Art Deco era. Oddly, the stately Secretariat Building, which houses the U.N.'s office workers, seems to glorify bureaucracy, rather than diplomacy; the blind-walled General Assembly lurks like a Nautilus submarine at the foot of the slab.

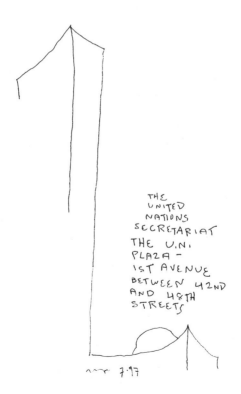

THE UNITED NATIONS SECRETARIAT
THE U.N. PLAZA –
1ST AVENUE
BETWEEN 42ND AND 48TH STREETS

7.97

LEVER HOUSE

390 Park Avenue bet. East 53rd and East 54th Streets
1952, Gordon Bunshaft

rchitect Gordon Bunshaft of Skidmore, Owings & Merrill was one of the most prolific innovators and one of the greatest showmen of the 1950s and 1960s. He was to the glass box what Raymond Hood was to Art Deco, or Stanford White to the Gilded Age. Bunshaft forever changed the look of Park Avenue, and indeed, cityscapes around the world, with the introduction of his small office building sheathed in glass.

Lever House is a vision in miniature of postwar America. The 24-story office tower stands on a full block of Park Avenue as if it were isolated in a suburban glade. Lever employees can park in an underground garage, eat in the third-floor company cafeteria and drive home without ever having to set foot on a city street. (They once even played shuffleboard on the landscaped terrace outside the glass doors of the cafeteria.) Lever House also has the distinction of being one of the earliest fully climate-controlled buildings, with sealed windows, so employees don't even have to breathe the same air as city dwellers.

Supported entirely from within by steel frame construction, the glass walls seem to float on stainless steel columns above a ground floor courtyard. The building's sil-houette is a pure abstraction: a vertical slab stands weightlessly above and to one side of a horizontal slab. The sense that these are pure volumes without mass is heightened by the open space between the slabs at the third floor. There is a wonderful interplay of solids and space: an open-sided, covered area leads to the hollow square of the courtyard open to the sky. Glass

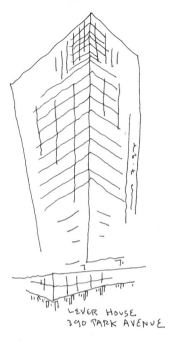

LEVER HOUSE
390 PARK AVENUE

walls separate the interior space of the lobby from the courtyard, but the visual effect is of uninterrupted space.

In the 1950s, Lever House's shiny stainless steel and ethereal blue-green glass provided a brand-new image for corporate America. The look has been copied to the point where glass buildings are no longer noteworthy, but Lever House still stands out because of its sublime proportions. Its open design, however, has never been copied because it is highly impractical from a purely commercial point of view. The total floor space of the tower is a minuscule 22,000 square feet—about half the square footage of a single floor of the World Trade Center (p.88).

SEAGRAM BUILDING

375 Park Avenue bet. East 52nd and East 53rd Streets
1958, Ludwig Mies van der Rohe and Philip Johnson

Besides Lever House, Park Avenue's other celebrated glass box is the Seagram Building, which actually hides a secret. Behind the 30-story tower stands an 11-story, T-shaped "bustle" where most of the office space, and the Four Seasons restaurant, is hidden. (In fact, many of the Seagram's offices do not even have windows.) With the Seagram as a model, later developers reproduced this basic layout at less cost but also less elegantly, not exactly what Mies van der Rohe meant when he said, "Less is more."

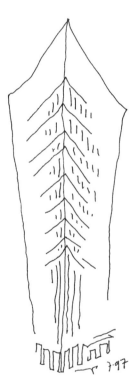

The Seagram is far superior to what came after it because it distills Classical architecture to its minimalist essence. The 100-by-200-foot pink granite plaza is like the forecourt of a Greek temple in that it sets up the viewer for the full experience of the structure. Like Doric columns, the bronze I-beams that run the full length of the façade provide a play of light and shadow. Verd antique, mottled green marble parapets (which make excellent benches, one of the reasons the plaza is so popular) are a concise reference to a Classical material. In fact, the green marble together with the white travertine walls, used for separating the plaza from the street, made for a color combination that became an instant classic, and a symbol for Modernism, copied everywhere from coffee shops to hotel and apartment lobbies, in the same way that aqua and rose became the colors of Postmodernism in the 1980s.

Although the Seagram represents a machine-age aesthetic of unadorned, basic materials, in reality it is a consummate hand-made art object. Almost everything about the building had to be custom made, including the extraordinary, miniature bronze I-beams that lend a sculptural clarity of detail to the façade, and the special bronze-colored glass. The building's bronze metal skin must be oiled by hand every year to keep it from turning the color of the Statue of Liberty.

People are naturally drawn to the Seagram plaza's mix of Classical serenity and Modernist energy. The pink granite floor sweeps uninterruptedly through the glass envelope of the lobby (an idea taken from Frank Lloyd Wright), so that the distinction between interior and exterior dissolves. The horizontal plane of the plaza and the soaring vertical of the tower meld imperceptibly, lending a charged air to the space around the building.

UNION CARBIDE BUILDING

(now Chemical Bank)

270 Park Avenue bet. East 47th and East 48th Streets
1960, Natalie de Blois

The aesthetic of Minimalism is by nature understated, so many of its best effects tend to be almost invisible. A fine line separates the great from the banal. The Union Carbide Building is such a bold Minimalist statement that you might almost overlook it.

The façade and the plaza of the 41-story building both are often dismissed as lesser versions of those of the Seagram Building (page 72), which to some extent is true. The façade's protruding black steel I-beams are not as finely detailed as the bronze ones of the Seagram, and the truncated gray granite plaza is remarkably user-unfriendly (there's no place to sit).

On the other hand, the grandly scaled, three-story glass-walled lobby is a Minimalist masterpiece. Natalie de Blois, one of the few women in the Internationalist boys club, and interior designer Jack G. Dunbar applied a breathtakingly Minimalist palette to this vast space. The natural colors of the materials visually separate the elements of the lobby: gray granite for the floor, clear glass for the walls, and stainless steel for the interior trim. The supporting steel columns are matte black, and the ceiling is flat white. The only true color is in the bold red of the monumentally scaled walls that house the elevators in the central core of the building. Seen from the street, the transparent glass walls of the lobby seem to hold up the black building weightlessly. The hot red interior walls make the building look like a rocket ship on a launch pad with a burning flame below it.

The massive red-walled core and the empty space of the lobby are engaged in a dialogue: the lobby is as full of empty space as it is full of the core. The building's glass skin, especially at night, seems to disappear altogether, and the space around the core becomes tangible, not just as an absence but as a kind of active presence, a force. The building poses a question: is a glass building a solid or a void? The answer: a little of both.

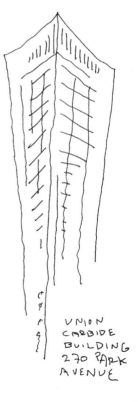

UNION
CARBIDE
BUILDING
270 PARK
AVENUE

PAN AM BUILDING

(now MetLife Building)

**200 Park Avenue bet. East 45th and East 46th Streets
1963, Emery Roth & Sons, Pietro Belluschi,
and Walter Gropius**

The Pan Am Building is everybody's favorite building to hate: it's too big, it has no connection with the surrounding buildings, and it blocks the sky over Park Avenue, like a stray iceberg. Everything about it is huge: 66 elevators and 2.4 million square feet of office space spread over 55 stories, the most floor space of any office building in the world when it opened.

THE PAN-AM
(ONCE) NOW
MET LIFE
PARK AVENUE · BETWEEN
45TH AND 46TH

The whole thing would never have caused so much controversy if Gropius and Belluschi had not turned the slab 90 degrees from the original plan so that it blotted out the sky. Seen from 44th Street, the elongated octagon succeeds more as a tower than as a slab. Because the building defied the traditional grid street plan of Manhattan by standing athwart the avenue, it became a symbol of the Internationalists' disdain for cities.

Time has not mellowed the Pan Am's unlovely, pre- cast concrete façade. The bulky concrete mullions are a crude joke compared with the hand-tooled perfection of the Seagram Building (page 72), or the sculptural splendor of Grand Central Terminal. Still, on the positive side, the building is, if nothing else, a monument to the mega scaled efficiency of postwar America. It is a Modernist dream of transportation: all hard surfaces in the pedestrian concourse, whooshing escalators, and speeding elevators. Helicopters once landed on the Pan Am's roof port, "like a dragonfly on a tomb" as Joni Mitchell sang, until 1977, when a landing strut on one of the helicopters collapsed, resulting in the death of four passengers and a pedestrian on the street.

The second-level car ports on the Pershing Viaduct, the bridge that connects the two ends of Park Avenue, are among the truly serene places in the city, with interesting second-story views of midtown and the skyscrapers that form a giant wall around Grand Central. The gliding descent on the escalators from the hyper-Modernist concourse of the Pan Am Building down to the sun-dappled vault of Grand Central makes for a study in contrast that is one of my favorite in the city, a Postmodern experience in itself.

CBS BUILDING

51 West 52nd Street at Avenue of the Americas
1965, Eero Saarinen & Associates

The CBS Building is the only skyscraper designed by the Finnish architect Eero Saarinen, who is better known for his low, organically shaped structures, such as the TWA Terminal at J.F.K. The CBS Building was nicknamed "Black Rock" because its sleek vertical lines of projecting granite piers seem to form parapets at the roofline, giving the tower a strong neo-Gothic feel. The jagged top looks as if it had been cropped with a pair of pinking shears.

The 35-story tower combines elements of the early, tall masonry buildings and Modern steel and glass skyscrapers. Unlike most Modern buildings, the CBS is not simply a covered steel cage. Instead, the beams run from a central elevator core to an exterior frame of granite-clad concrete piers. The piers support the building the way masonry walls held buildings up before the advent of the steel frame. As a result, the interior of the CBS is completely free of columns, thus allowing 800,000 square feet of unobstructed space.

The appearance of this Modernist tower very much depends on where you stand in relation to it. There is a brilliant dialogue between solids and space going on here: the giant piers support the building like the fingers of a hand, but at the same time the gray glass windows between the piers function as a skin. From oblique angles, the façade can look like a solid stone monolith, but as you walk around the tower, the walls ripple and bristle with energy as the piers seem to open and collapse like accordion pleats.

CBS BUILDING
52ND STREET
AND 6TH
AVENUE

7·97

In keeping with the Gothic theme, the sunken plaza resembles a moat more than a public place, but emphasizes the free-standing, sculptural nature of the tower. The lobby, in dark gray granite and white travertine, is stark to the point of being hostile. The subterranean door to the messenger center off the plaza looks like the entrance to a tomb, perhaps a little too Gothic.

SILVER TOWERS

100 and 110 Bleecker Street, and 505 LaGuardia Place
1966, I.M. Pei

When my family lived at Silver Towers, my stepfather always insisted on entering the grounds by taking the long way around—going up the steps on LaGuardia Place and passing the three identical 30-story concrete buildings in a stately procession, rather than just cutting across the driveway. Lately, I have realized that the long way around is an important Modernist experience.

Modern buildings explore the relationship between solids and the flow and perception of space, while Classical buildings treat space as a void, or negative, in opposition to the building's mass. Often, Modern buildings set up a Classical system, in this case the guided circulation through the plaza, typical of the Beaux-Arts style, and then comment upon the tradition. As you walk along the route at Silver Towers, you experience the changing relationships between the buildings and the flow of space around them. Classical buildings are complete in themselves; Modern buildings require an observer to form the relations and complete the picture. The grouping of the three towers is an exercise in relativity: with a small leap of imagination, the towers themselves seem to be moving through space rather than the observer.

The towers are arranged in a pinwheel fashion around a central court containing a 36-foot high, 60-ton concrete head of a woman, called Portrait of Sylvette. It is an interpretation by the Norwegian sculptor Carl Nesjar of a two-foot-tall metal sculpture by Picasso. The head, fragmented into Cubist planes, emphasizes the intent of the surrounding buildings to be seen as free-standing concrete sculptures. When Silver Towers opened, neighborhood kids immediately recognized the set-up for what it really is: the ultimate handball court, which accounts for the discreet no ball-playing signs.

100, 110 BLEECKER STREET AND 505 LA-GUARDIA PL.

MARINE MIDLAND BANK

**140 Broadway bet. Liberty and Cedar Streets
to Nassau Street
1967, Gordon Bunshaft**

Perhaps more than any other architect since Raymond Hood, Gordon Bunshaft understood the dual nature of skyscrapers as commerce and art. His 52-story Marine Midland Bank manages to exist both as a basic business commodity—rental space—and as an artistic image. The Marine's super-flat, transparent skin plainly proclaims its function as a container for commercial space. But at the same time, the façade of matte-finished black aluminum and dark bronze-tinted glass, which deviates only by two inches from sheer flatness, appears as weightless and two-dimensional as a purely geometric figure. The reflecting surface can appear as an abstract rhomboid, depending on your perspective.

Isamu Noguchi's twenty-eight-foot tall sculpture of a tilted, elongated red cube, which stands in front of the building on the Broadway side, is a key to understanding how the entire composition of building, cube, and plaza work together in sculptural terms. If the whole ensemble were a piece of music, it might be called "Variations on an Elongated Cube."

The white travertine plaza runs all the way to the curb, eliminating a sidewalk, and takes up the entire, irregularly shaped city block. It's as if a white canvas were being stretched and pulled, like an Ellsworth Kelly painting. There are many levels of illusion at work here: Noguchi's sculpture is not really a cube—it's a rhombohedron. The stretched cube looks as if it is being pulled into three dimensions from the two-dimensional surface of the plaza. The black building itself is a wonderful synthesis of the plaza and the cube, because its "footprint," or floor plan, is not a rectangle at all, but a trapezoid. The Nassau Street

140 BROADWAY
BETWEEN
LIBERTY
AND CEDAR
9-4-97

façade is four bays (or window groupings) wide, and tapers to three bays on the Broadway side. The unusual acute and oblique angles that result heighten the building's appearance as a flat plane rather than a container of space.

The building brilliantly explores the Modernist tension between the surface and volume of a cube. In a classical building, the profile is the most certain and stable aspect. Bunshaft reverses this: in the Marine Midland, the space inside is stable, but the appearance of the building's wrapper depends on your point of view.

Bunshaft was a collector of Modern Art and was familiar with the Abstract Expressionist movement in painting, which sought to dispose of conventions such as naturalist images, perspective, and the illusion of a third dimension, to concentrate on the medium itself—the flat surface, the properties of pigment, and the material that supports the pigment. Similarly, Bunshaft reduced his palette to a minimalist red, white, and black to explore the architecture of pure, flat planes.

EXXON BUILDING

1251 Avenue of the Americas
bet. West 49th and West 50th Streets
1971, Harrison, Abramovitz & Harris

MCGRAW-HILL BUILDING

1221 Avenue of the Americas
bet. West 48th and West 49th Streets
1972, Harrison, Abramovitz & Harris

CELANESE BUILDING

1211 Avenue of the Americas
bet. West 47th and West 48th Streets
1973, Harrison, Abramovitz & Harris

This strip of three nearly identical skyscrapers most says "New York" to me—the glamorous, urbane world of *Desk Set, The Man in the Gray Flannel Suit,* and *How to Succeed in Business Without Really Trying*—even though all of these movies were made well before the first tower went up in 1971.

This is pin-stripe, button-down commercial architecture at its best. The three slabs were named the XYZ buildings in the planning stages, because of the near interchangeability of their heights (all three are 54 stories), general configuration, and similar vertically striped stone and glass façades. The basic design is a variation of the Time-Life Building next door at 1271 Avenue of the Americas, built by the same firm in 1959. As an ensemble, the towers blend elegantly into the urban fabric, rather than overwhelming it, despite their huge scale.

THE
EXXON
BUILDING
6TH AVENUE
BETWEEN
49TH AND
50TH

Something about the way the light reflects off the narrow vertical glass ribbons of the windows, and the uplifted V's of the cantilevered canopies, makes me think of the hopefulness and optimism of the Modernist movement. The limestone façades of numbers 1211 and

1251 are a nod to, and a crisp update of, the vertical limestone stripes on the older Rockefeller Center across the avenue (1221 is faced in a light, purple granite that subtly repeats the granite base trim of the Rockefeller Center buildings).

Inside the plate-glass doors of the XYZ towers lies an idealized version of city life—clean, secure, pleasant, efficient. The Celanese Building, the last of the three to be built, is the most artfully realized. It is also the most accessible, because it has an entrance directly on the avenue. Step inside, and immediately the air in the marble lobby is a little cooler, the light softer, and the sound muffled. I rather like the *Citizen Kane* scale of the oversized, marble-paved, and wood-paneled corridor.

Whatever their shortcomings, the XYZ towers are extraordinarily well used. You see people everywhere, at every level, like the figures in the Oskar Schlemmer painting *Bauhaus Stairway*. Together, they create a city inside a city, with such anomalies as a "sidewalk" cafe with little tables below street level. The complex is thoroughly integrated with the subway, and with the maze of corridors under Rockefeller Center. The dozens of stores do not advertise above ground, so that the corridors have the feel of a private club.

1 WORLD TRADE CENTER

Church to West Street

1973, Minoru Yamasaki and Emery Roth & Sons

2 WORLD TRADE CENTER

Liberty to Vesey Street

1974, Minoru Yamasaki and Emery Roth & Sons

Not even a remake of *King Kong*, Philippe Petit on a tightrope, or an attack by mad bombers could endear these twin aluminum and glass behemoths to old-time New Yorkers. But for the generation born after they were built, it is a different story, and the twin towers appear on tour bus logos and posters for the Rangers and Yankees, in the Channel 11 logo, and on such tourist gimcracks as thermometers, pencil sharpeners, and key chains.

By any stretch of the imagination, the 1,350-foot, 110-story towers, together containing an astonishing 10 million square feet of floor space (ten times that of the Empire State Building), do not belong on the skyline. (Each floor of each building represents an entire *acre* of office space.) The towers threaten to upend the whole island of Manhattan, but after more than twenty years, they seem to blend into the woodwork just like every other assault on the sensibilities, such as the new Penn Station and the Pan Am Building.

The towers are something of an engineering marvel in that their exterior aluminum-clad steel columns actually hold up the buildings like rib cages, rather than internal frames. The columns are latticed together with cross beams to form a strong hollow tube. (A tube is the strongest, lightest structure in nature: consider, for example, the long bones in your body, or the stalk of a plant.) In an oddly decorative touch for such ungainly buildings, the piers, which run right down to

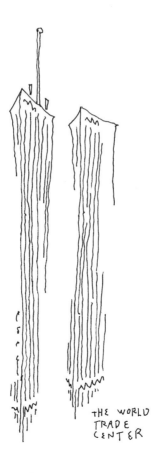

THE WORLD
TRADE
CENTER

the sidewalk, taper into pointed Venetian Gothic arches at the top and bottom.

Each tower has about 43,600 windows, just twenty-two inches wide, so that glass makes up only 30 percent of the building's surface. At the time of their construction, the towers were the tallest buildings in the world, and it was thought that their tenants would experience vertigo if the windows were any larger (the buildings do sway up to twelve feet off center in a gale). On a clear day, you can see almost forever from the 107th-floor observatory at 2 World Trade Center: maximum visibility is up to 35 miles. The more adventurous can try the open-air rooftop promenade on the 110th floor, weather permitting. Admission is four dollars.

The fact that there are two towers adds a kind of surreal dimension. Together, they function like a minimalist sculpture in that they constantly change in relation to each other. The towers do not stand side by side, but rather on an angle to each other, so that one always appears in the foreground and the other, smaller, in the background. Their shiny aluminum skins also have a wonderfully sculptural quality, reflecting the moods of the sky at different times of day.

W. R. GRACE BUILDING

1114 Avenue of the Americas (41 West 42nd Street)
1974, Gordon Bunshaft

9 WEST 57TH STREET

bet. 5th and 6th Avenues
1974, Gordon Bunshaft

The ski-shaped, sloped façades of the 50-story black glass and white travertine tower at 9 West 57th Street, and its near twin, the 47-story Grace Building, are among the most recognizable profiles in the city, but here Modernism begins to stretch at the seams. At some level, architect Gordon Bunshaft must have begun to tire of the inflexibility of the International Style, and was searching for a way to put some fun back into architecture.

If so, he succeeded. Anyone who sees either tower for the first time usually does a double take, because the concavely curved façades exaggerate the sense that a building is looming over you. Bunshaft arrived at the shape by using smoothly curved setbacks, rather than the usual bumpy ones. You can't help but giggle at the vertigo-inducing effect.

In both towers, the piers become columns and pierce the travertine-covered street-level canopies at a jaunty angle, like the legs of a 1950s davenport. The columns, which come right down to each tower's

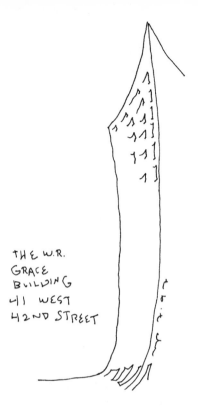

THE W.R.
GRACE
BUILDING
41 WEST
42ND STREET

white travertine plaza, heighten the sloping effect. The blocky slabs, however, are rather uninteresting when seen from any angle other than directly below. From the side, they look like a cartoon character dodging a bullet.

After a career of pushing the minimalist aesthetic of the International Style to its limits with such masterworks as Lever House, and Marine Midland, and Chase Manhattan Plaza (pp. 70, and 82), it appears as if Bunshaft longed for the theatricality of past skyscrapers like the Chanin (page 42) and the Chrysler (page 50), which sought to dazzle the man in the street. Perhaps he felt that Internationalism was misunderstood and overlooked by the public, or perhaps he just felt the style was exhausted.

The tower at 9 West 57th Street features such odd, retro details as a giant stainless steel "woggle," (a rounded, abstract decorative element) above the closed-off escalators that go underground. It is almost as if Bunshaft were anticipating the spirited hijinx of the Postmodern movement by returning to the past.

The askew reflection in 9 West's curving black glass façade of the giant, polychrome Napoleonic medallion that crowns 29 West 57th Street next door is an interesting symbol of the relationship of contemporary buildings to ornamental styles of the past. Old styles have been picked up again, but their context is something new.

1 AND 2 UNITED NATIONS PLAZA

East 44th Street at First Avenue
1976 and 1983, Kevin Roche John Dinkeloo & Assocs.

One fine day in the East Village, I looked up First Avenue and saw what appeared to be a big blue cube floating on the horizon. Surely it was an optical illusion—there was nothing so big and so blue in midtown. I looked for it again on other days, but the big blue cube was gone. It was unnerving until I figured out that what I had seen was the all-glass wall of the United Nations Plaza reflecting an unusually clear blue sky in New York.

It's just this kind of atmospherics—the shifting play of light and reflection on a reflective surface—that makes glass buildings so interesting as free-standing sculptural objects. Glass gives very little idea of a building's actual mass, and in U.N. Plaza we see an early version of the Postmodernist idea that a building and its façade can be two separate entities, rather than unified as in the Classical and Modernist styles. Here, this discontinuity is heightened because the grid patterns on the outside of the two 39-story buildings actually have no direct relation to the floors behind them. The levels on the grids are not set in the one-to-one correspondence you would expect, so there is no real way to tell from the outside something as basic as how tall the buildings are.

The towers resemble crisp, weightless sheets of folded paper. Their light-colored vertical and horizontal gridding resembles the lines on a piece of draftsman's paper—a Postmodern tip of the hat to a building's origins as a two-dimensional abstraction. From some angles directly below, the façades seems to have no width at all. My favorite illusion is to see lighted rooms with walls that appear no thicker than a sheet of paper. The mass of the buildings is completely disguised by this illusion of origami in glass.

The two buildings are wonderfully appropriate to this neighborhood of diplomats. To anthropomorphize them, something we inevitably do to the buildings we live with, they resemble two speakers in colloquy, one leaning in to emphasize a point. They also represent a new understanding of the role of the tall tower: No. 1 was the first building in New York to combine office space with ten floors of hotel rooms at the top. A similar plan is being looked at to save the debt-ridden Chrysler Building.

CITICORP CENTER

Lexington Avenue bet. East 53rd and East 54th Streets
1977, Hugh Stubbins

The silvery, 59-story Citicorp Center, with its distinctive triangular crown, is New York's first Postmodernist skyscraper. It defies such basic assumptions of Modernism as that form follows function, and that ornamentation is superfluous.

Judging by appearances, the Citicorp's structure is a mystery. Just what holds the thing up? Unlike the earliest building in this book, the Bayard-Condict (page 10), where the façade clearly shows how the weight is supported, the Citicorp's slick aluminum and glass wrapper reveals little of what is going on inside.

Citicorp is actually a hollow tube, lashed together by X-shaped girders. These reinforcing girders, which act as wind-braces so that the building is not deformed by the force of high winds, are in turn hidden behind aluminum panels that are flush with the reflecting windows. The building perches high above the ground on the legs of four "supercolumns." The open, 114-foot-tall base, in combination with the skin that reflects light and sky, makes the Citicorp seem almost ethereal.

The Citicorp's purely ornamental top is its most daring deviation from the no-frills orthodoxy of the International Style. The 161-foot-tall crown, in the form of a perfect triangle, is one of the most easily recognizable in the thicket of anonymous buildings in midtown, yet it is completely unnecessary from a structural point of view. The original idea in the energy-conscious 1970s was to use the angled roof for solar panels. When this proved unfeasible, architect Hugh Stubbins decided to keep the distinctive shape sheerly for design's sake. It was time to put visual excitement back into architecture.

Citicorp Center also anticipated Postmodernism's increasing sensitivity to the urban environment. It is a very large building—1,780,000 square feet—but it does not overwhelm the neighborhood. The plaza leading down to the subway is one of the most used in the city, and Saint Peter's Lutheran Church, nestled at the foot of the tower, thrives in its new hyper-Modern surroundings.

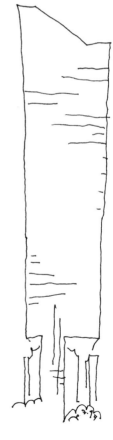

TRUMP TOWER

725 Fifth Avenue at East 56th Streets
1983, Der Scutt and Swanke Hayden Connell

Trump Tower is an unabashed temple to conspicuous consumption. The six-story, skylit atrium lobby can be viewed as the 1980s equivalent of a Gilded Age interior, meant to celebrate the affluence of its occupants.

Everything about the Trump lobby bespeaks wealth, from the gorgeously glowing, apricot-colored Breccia Pernice marble from Italy to the polished brass panels and tinted mirrors that flatter its visitors. (I still can't figure out how they keep the brass railings so free of fingerprints.) Tail-coated doormen oversee this gleaming grotto.

As befits its bustling Fifth Avenue location, the tower is a mixed use (residential and commercial) building. Condominiums sold for $10 million when the building opened in 1983, and attracted such celebrities as Steven Spielberg, Michael Jackson, and Johnny Carson. The low-lit, black-marble-lined residential entrance on East 56th Street is a model of privacy and exclusivity. The slick, black glass exterior features busy setbacks, at the lower levels planted with a V-shaped formation of illuminated trees and ivy.

In many ways the Trump resembles a mall that caters to the rich, what with its skylight and mirrored escalators, a fountain cascading down one marble wall, and an underground food court. One thing that has made the Trump so successful where many urban malls have failed is the mix of stores. Here are some of the most luxurious names in retail—Ferragamo, Cartier, Coach, and Harry Winston. The atrium now connects to the Nike super-store on East 57th Street, which in turn connects to the bamboo-planted I.B.M. atrium on Madison Avenue.

The Trump is one of New York's greatest tourist attractions. The lobby is always filled with browsers. Christmas time is especially festive, with the balconies decked with wreaths and carolers in the lobby.

56TH AND
5TH AVENUE

AT&T BUILDING

(now Sony Building)

550 Madison Avenue bet. East 55th and East 56th Streets
1984, Philip Johnson and John Burgee

Philip Johnson, once the high priest of high Modernism, switched hats to become the court jester of Postmodernism. His 42-story tower sheathed in pink granite acted as a lightning rod to attract attention to the Postmodernist movement.

Johnson's aim was to subvert Internationalism's sterility, a condition he calls "glass box-itis." The AT&T's top is a wonderful, gratuitous gesture, literally placing style for style's sake above everything. The grandly overstated broken pediment, which reminded many of the signature curve of a Chippendale highboy, was a trumpet call to reintegrate historicism into Modernism. For the AT&T, Johnson resurrected the stone façade (and almost single-handedly the quarrying industry) with 1.3 million square feet of Stony Creek, Connecticut pink granite.

The AT&T borrowed from the past with its Chippendale top and Romanesque entryway, but these were built on a scale that had never been seen before. They were not just imitations of Classical forms, but a unique interpretation. By making the decorative elements so large, and applying them out of context, Johnson has made us consider how important deco-

ration is in forming a
building's image.

The proportions of
the building have been
criticized, but I think this is the point. The shallow, drafting-board
feel of the elevations adds to the effect of the building as theorem.
The building has little sense of mass because of the shallow window reveals, and seems to have jumped off the architect's drawing board. The oversized entryway is in keeping with the stretchy
scale of the building, which rises straight up from the street, relin-
quishing a base. The stretching effect is surprising and kind of
funny. But as we all know, buildings aren't supposed to be funny.
I think Johnson was just trying to inject a much needed light note.

Illusion and reality are reversed here: the reality of the AT&T's
façade recedes into illusion because of its extraordinarily flat, schematic elevations. At the same time, the ornamentation becomes substantial
because of the three-dimensional articulation of the arch and the projecting cornice of the Chippendale top.

When the building was completed, many critics felt that Johnson
was thumbing his nose at the architectural world, but now that time has
mellowed the design, and the Chippendale top has settled into the skyline, the AT&T is a recognizable and welcome neighbor.

LIPSTICK BUILDING

885 Third Avenue bet. East 53rd and East 54th Streets
1986, John Burgee and Philip Johnson

Popularly known as the Lipstick Building because of its distinctive shape of telescoping ellipses, this 34-story tower evokes the romantic skyscrapers of the 1930s. Dusky rose colored granite, red-brown opaque glass, and sinuous lines recall an ocean liner's smokestack or the streamlined lobby of the original McGraw-Hill Building (page 60). The ribbon windows arranged in bands evoke Frank Lloyd Wright's hyper-Moderne Johnson Wax Research Tower in Racine, Wisconsin.

Returning to the curved line was perhaps Johnson's ultimate heresy against the orthodoxy of Mies van der Rohe. The Internationalists championed rectilinear forms precisely to do away with such odd designs. The Lipstick is truly anarchistic because the setbacks are not centered, so the entire structure seems to wobble and shimmy like wrist bangles. (Like the Seagram [page 72], the shape of the Lipstick is a bit of sleight-of-hand; the main elevator core and much of the office space are hidden in a "bustle" that connects to the lobby.)

Postmodern architecture embraces disjunctures, rather than trying to impose a uniform style. The flared granite capitals of the Lipstick's columns do not quite touch or fit under the stainless steel lip of the building, and bulge out at odd angles to emphasize their decorative rather than strictly structural function. The panels of polished red Swedish Imperial granite that make up the columns are assembled with obvious cement seams and are not perfectly flush, which dispels the idea that the stone is structural. Rather than pretending to be stone columns, these columns reveal their artifice.

At every point, Burgee and Johnson have emphasized bumpiness and discontinuity, instead of integration. In a design of the 30s or the 50s, the brushed stainless steel bands around the building would have

been smooth, streamlined parabolas; here they are arranged in flat panels to show that these are square forms that will not easily resolve themselves into circles. The overall feel of the building is not that of the Classical repose of the Seagram, but instead of a jittery, off-the-cuff contemporaneity.

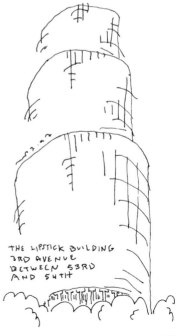

THE LIPSTICK BUILDING
3RD AVENUE
BETWEEN 53RD
AND 54TH

WORLD FINANCIAL CENTER

ONE WORLD FINANCIAL CENTER
(Dow Jones Building)
West Street opposite Cedar Street
1985, Cesar Pelli

THREE WORLD FINANCIAL CENTER
(American Express Headquarters)
West Street at Vesey Street
1985, Cesar Pelli

FOUR WORLD FINANCIAL CENTER
(Merrill Lynch Headquarters, north building)
Vesey Street at North End Avenue
1986, Cesar Pelli

TWO WORLD FINANCIAL CENTER
(Merrill Lynch Headquarters, south building)
West Street bet. Liberty and Vesey Streets
1987, Cesar Pelli

WINTER GARDEN
Bet. Two and Three World Financial Center
1988, Cesar Pelli

ostmodernism moves into a Classical phase with Cesar Pelli's elegantly scaled World Financial Center. These are handsome urban buildings, without the shock value of early Postmodernism. Theories of returning to historicism and incorporating discontinuity have become accepted parts of the architect's toolbox.

The vast, six-million-square-foot complex contains offices, stores such as Ann Taylor, Godiva, and Rizzoli, and restaurants and bars frequented by a young Wall Street crowd. The Winter Garden indoor plaza is the heart and soul of the complex. There is a wonderful sense of anticipation as you approach from the second level and see the elliptical space, lined with four colors of Italian marble,

open up before you. The Victorian-style, 120-foot tall barrel-vaulted steel and glass arch that frames a view of the harbor reminds me of something out of *20,000 Leagues Under the Sea*. Nearly the size of the concourse at Grand Central Terminal, the chamber is lined with a fresh crop of living columns of thirty-five-foot-high palm trees from Arizona. The Winter

THE WINTER GARDEN

Garden is home to some of the city's best free concert series, as well as the annual New York Orchid Show.

The four main towers of the Financial Center, which range in height from 34 to 51 stories, re-create the history of the skyscraper. As your eye travels upward, each of the four buildings shows a progressive movement from a predominantly granite base to a glass crown, just as tall buildings historically moved from stone to glass walls. Architect Cesar Pelli takes the history lesson into the Postmodern era by making the crowns sheerly decorative.

The towers celebrate architectural contradictions rather than attempting to conceal or unify them. At ground level, thin granite veneer arches stand right beside unconcealed steel columns that actually bear the weight. Depending upon your vantage point, the columns appear to be solid stone or a thin panel. Illusion and reality appear as equally valid aspects of the design.

The skin of the towers also plays with the contradictions of a façade. Deep reveals, which seem to show massively thick walls, are set directly below flush glass windows that make the walls seem to have no weight at all. Which is real? Both? Neither? The two images are contradictory, but stand side by side.

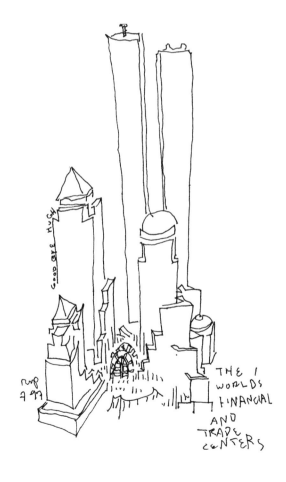

425 LEXINGTON AVENUE

bet. East 43rd and East 44th Streets
1988, Helmut Jahn

Imagine you have just received a commission to build a 31-story tower at the foot of one of the most famous skyscrapers in the world. Would you try to compete with the crown of the Chrysler Building, or ignore it? Helmut Jahn, who built Philadelphia's One Liberty Place, a wonderful retro granite and glass tribute to the Chrysler

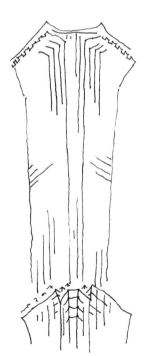

Building, takes neither tack.

Here he displays the sly wit of Postmodernism, undermining the paradigm of the setback skyscraper by making his tower mushroom out at the top. The design has historical roots in the 1314 Palazzo Vecchio in Florence, but there is nothing else quite like it in New York.

Jahn's tower is not so much a tribute to the Chrysler as to the Pan Am Building (page 76), of all things! I can't help but smile when I see the two together from East 44th Street—425 Lexington seems to be leaning into the frame and literally tipping its hat to its monstrous Internationalist predecessor. It's as if Jahn is saying that fantasy in architecture is fine, but it's the severity of Internationalism that needs a little tweak.

The octagonal rose marble and aqua glass building combines the monumentality of the Italian Renaissance with the sleekness of glass architecture, embracing rather than trying to resolve the contradiction. The surface is busy and self-negating: heavy black granite corbels at the base and roof cornice appear to be pasted on, and deeply recessed windows are placed right next to windows that are flush with the wall. Are the walls made of heavy stone or thin glass? Everything is up for grabs here—the building is a pastiche of historical styles butting against each other without resolution.

I think what the big, 600,000-square-foot building does best is fit into the eclectic street scene on Lexington Avenue From just north, the block forms an exciting Postmodernist jumble, with the Italianate brick tower of 441 Lexington right next to the glass mushroom of 425, and the Deco gargoyles of the Chrysler Building staring out over the city. From a certain angle uptown, 425 reveals itself as a platform and pedestal for the Chrysler Building, which emerges like a pistil from its petals. Seen from downtown, the glass crown of 425 tilts out at the same angle and at almost the same height as the winged urns on the Chrysler.

WORLDWIDE PLAZA

West 49th Street to West 50th Streets
bet. Eighth and Ninth Avenues
1989, apartment towers, Frank Williams;
office tower, Skidmore, Owings & Merrill

Worldwide Plaza, comprising a 48-story office tower and a 39-story apartment building, is a Postmodernist return to the romantic skyscraper of the 1930s. While the Internationalists mandated flat roofs, Postmodern architects are not afraid to admit that Americans prefer buildings with a recognizable top as a change from buildings with all the personality of up-ended shoeboxes.

The copper-topped rose and beige brick office tower melds many historical styles: its translucent crown is made of frosted glass set in an aluminum frame, lit from within by a beacon, in the German Expressionist tradition. In the Deco style, the eight-sided copper pyramid below the pinnacle is largely ornamental, rather than functional. (The actual roof of the building is a flat, waterproof surface on the forty-eighth floor.) The copper top, now the color of an old penny, will turn green over the years, a reference to the colorful crowns of the 1930s, and to the decorative copper roofs of earlier skyscrapers like the Woolworth Building (page 22). The crown (echoed on a smaller scale on the apartment tower) also recalls the neoclassical dormered roofs of early eclectic tall buildings.

With its chamfered corners, regular fenestration, and setbacks accented in white brick, the office tower is in the stone skyscraper tradition of the American Radiator Building (page 30). In contrast, the apartment building at its foot is open and glassy in the International Style, a Postmodern commentary on the arbitrariness of style.

The open plaza gives the picket-shaped office tower the impact of a NASA liftoff. The effect is heightened at night, when gases from the heating, ventilation, and air-conditioning system drift in the light of the illuminated nosecone. By the way, the block on which Worldwide Plaza stands has some rich historical associations that are now all but lost—from 1925 to 1966, it was the site of the second Madison Square Garden, where boxing legends such as Joe Louis and Floyd Patterson slugged it out.

BERTELSMANN BUILDING

1540 Broadway at 45th Street
1990, Skidmore, Owings & Merrill

Amid the visual overload of Times Square, you might not even notice the 45-story green and blue glass tower that stands at the "bowtie" of the intersection. If you do look up, you might think it isn't quite finished yet because of the skeletal "prow" of steel girders at the top, but this is an example of Deconstructivism, in which conventions such as the full curtain wall are taken apart. The prow is also appropriate for Times Square because it resembles the scaffolding of a billboard.

The Bertelsmann Building, which houses the subterranean Virgin Megastore, and the publisher, Bantam-Doubleday-Dell, is very much an office building suited to Times Square. The jagged prow on top was originally conceived as a kind of signature billboard for the building, much like the signs all over the square. The crown, framed in open steel beams that look unfinished, rises like a flèche, or slender spire, on a medieval cathedral. The neo-Gothic effect is completed by dark glass piers that rise to the roofline like parapets. The building's triangular nose on the Broadway side adds a distinctive profile, although the lobby entrance is actually on 45th Street. The two-color glass sheath of the whole structure gives the illusion of a light green building emerging from a darker blue one. Slight variations in the depth of the façade add to this effect.

The base of the building dissolves into an incredible hodgepodge of billboards and neon signs, which seem to climb up the building like lichen on a tree. On the 45th Street side, the low, blank-faced base continues the cornice line of the extravagant Beaux-Arts façade of the Lyceum Theater, the oldest legitimate playhouse in the city, but makes no attempt to integrate it. The Broadway side of the Bertelsmann makes

even less sense: here it accommodates a run-down, three-story brick building at 1550, hidden behind a steaming billboard for Eight O'Clock Roast coffee. Times Square created a Postmodern discontinuity of images well ahead of its time.

The virtual architecture of moving electronic signs has taken over Times Square. In some future scenario out of *Blade Runner*, perhaps electronic fronts will replace stone façades entirely. Then, the look of a building could change weekly or even hourly instead of every decade.

712 FIFTH AVENUE

bet. 55th and 56th Streets
1991, Kohn Pedersen Fox

In a well-composed picture, not everything can be in the foreground. Postmodernists, who are more sensitive to a building's urban context than the Internationalists were, realize that the same holds true for cities. This subtly colored, slender campanile is distinguished not so much by how it stands out on the cityscape, but rather how well it fits into it. The 55-story office building accomplishes three seemingly disparate goals: it preserves the historic Fifth Avenue block front, interweaves elements of most of the surrounding architecture into its façade, and still makes a distinct and individual architectural statement.

The tower, set back 55 feet from the line of the street, appears to float behind the low-scaled buildings on Fifth Avenue. Its nearly flat façade reduces the sense of mass so that it appears to be weightless. The five-story limestone entrance continues the traditional cornice line of the street and blends in perfectly with preexisting buildings, such as the white travertine façade of the Harry Winston jewelry shop on the corner.

With its uninterrupted limestone piers, the façade of 712 Fifth evokes Rockefeller Center to the south. By incorporating chunky accents of rough-finished brownstone, the façade also echoes the venerable brownstone Fifth Avenue Presbyterian Church, at the corner of Fifth Avenue and West 55th Street The tower's flat, squared-off crown even seems to match the high Modernism of Gordon Bunshaft's 9 West 57th Street (page 91).

Twelve etched glass panels of neoclassical zodiac figures above the entrance recall the extraordinary René Lalique–etched windows of the former Coty Building (now Henri Bendel) on Fifth Avenue, which look especially festive illuminated from within at night. Bendel has been preserved and incorporated as part of the base, and connects through with the lobby of 712 Fifth.

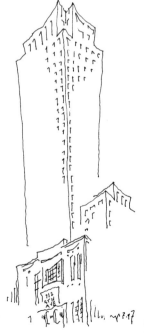

Panels of white Vermont marble and bronze medallions in grid patterns give the building a distinctive look, at the same time echoing the gilded panels of the Crown Building across West 56th Street Historical uses of color, texture, and ornament in the surrounding buildings have been reintegrated at 712 Fifth Avenue not as a quotation but as a vibrant contemporary architectural statement.

GLOSSARY

Art Deco: a design style that made its debut at the Exposition des Arts Décoratifs in Paris in 1925, and that grafted the streamlined aesthetic of the machine onto neoclassical motifs. Example: the Empire State Building (page 52).

Bay: a grouping of windows.

Bracket: an architectural support projecting from a wall.

Buttress: a projecting stone support built against a wall to reinforce it.

Beaux-Arts: a nineteenth-century style, taught at the Ecole des Beaux-Arts in Paris, which emphasizes clarity of layout and function, and reduces use of classical ornamentation. Example: the main branch of the New York Public Library on Fifth Avenue.

Campanile: a free-standing bell tower.

Capital: the top of a column. Classical columns are in the Doric style, a simple top; the Ionic style, with ornamental scrolls; and the Corinthian, decorated with an elaborate acanthus leaf motif. A composite capital combines the latter two styles.

Caryatid: a supporting column in the shape of a female figure.

Chamfer: a beveled edge or corner.

Classical: the styles of ancient Greece and Rome.

Coffered: decorated with sunken panels.

Colonettes: slender, decorative columns.

Column: a slender, upright supporting structure.

Corbel: a piece that projects from a wall and supports another element, such as a balcony.

Cornice: the top edge of a wall or building.

Crenellated: notched, like the battlements of a fortress.

Cupola: a small dome on a roof.

Deconstructivism: a recent style that seeks to take apart and redefine basic architectural conventions, such as symmetry, interior vs. exterior, and structural vs. nonstructural. Example: the Bertelsmann Building (page 112).

Dormer: an upright window set in a sloping roof.

Eclectic: a nineteenth-and early twentieth-century style of skyscraper design, inspired by historical styles. Example: the Woolworth Building (page 22).

Elevation: a flat scale drawing of a building's façade or sides.

Façade: literally "face"—the exterior appearance of a building.

Fenestration: the arrangement of windows in a building.

Filigree: delicate, intertwined ornamental work.

German Expressionism: a style that emphasizes dramatic lighting and unusual angles. Example: the Cities Service Building (page 64).

Gilded: coated with a gold color.

Girder: structural horizontal beams.

Glazed brick: a process that adds color to the brickface; the most commonly seen colors are white, buff, orange, and black.

Gothic: a medieval style of elaborately decorative, perpendicular architecture; **Gothic Revival** was a nineteenth-century movement to copy the Gothic style, and **neo-Gothic** uses some Gothic elements in another style. Example: the RCA Victor Building (page 62) is neo-Gothic.

Granite: a very hard rock containing feldspar and quartz, usually white, pink or gray in color. May appear rough or highly polished.

I-beam: a steel beam that looks like the capital letter I in cross-section.

International Style/Internationalism: a worldwide, post–World War II style typified by such architects as Mies van der Rohe, who rejected all applied historicism. Example: the Seagram Building (page 00).

Limestone: a gray-colored sedimentary rock with an even texture that can be cut into blocks or sculpted.

Lombardy Revival: a style influenced by northern Italian Romanesque architecture.

Mansard: a roof with two slopes on each of its four sides, the lower slope steeper than the upper.

Marble: a hard, crystalline form of metamorphic limestone that comes in vivid colors, including sea green, butterscotch orange, blood red, and the most valuable, pure white. Marble may be veined or mottled with other colors. It takes a high polish and holds the finest sculptural edge.

Masonry: brick or stonework.

Minimalism: an offshoot of Modernism that sought to do away with artistic conventions and distill modern art down to its essence. Example: Marine Midland Bank (page 82).

Modernism: a twentieth-century style that rejected decorative styles of the past in favor of an emphasis on such basic architectural elements as volume, mass, and space. Example: the Barclay-Vesey Building (page 34).

Mullions: slender vertical bars dividing window panes.

Neoclassical: a revival or application of Classical motifs. Example: the Waldorf-Astoria (page 58).

Palazzo: a palatial building in Italian Renaissance style.

Parapet: a low protective wall on a roof.

Parti: a building's overall layout or concept.

Pediment: a triangular decoration above a door or roof.

Pier: a long, vertical element in the façade of a building.

Pilaster: a flat, decorative column.

Pinnacle: a small turret or spire.

Polychrome: decorated in several colors.

Postmodernism: a style that rejected Modernism's ahistoricism in favor of using past styles out of their original context. Example: the AT&T Building (now Sony) (page 100).

Renaissance: a style influenced by the architecture of Italy and Western Europe from 1400 to 1600, which emphasizes humanist scale, symmetry, and an adaptation of Classical order. Example: the Candler Building (page 24).

Reveal: the space between the outer edge of a wall and the frame of a door or window.

Romanesque: a style influenced by European architecture of the eleventh and twelfth centuries, characterized by round arches and massive masonry walls.

Rosette: a painted or sculpted circular motif with petals radiating from its center.

Round-headed window: a window with a semicircular arch at the top.

Setback: a steplike indentation of a wall.

Setback code of 1916: a zoning change that required tall buildings to step back at the upper stories, according to a formula, to permit more air and light to reach the street. The code influenced the setback silhouette of skyscrapers.

Slab: a broad, wafer-like design typical of the International Style that maximized the amount of window space in a building.

Spandrel: the wall space between the top of a window and the windowsill on the floor above.

Steel-frame skeleton: a construction method in which steel columns and girders are connected to support the weight of a building.

Terra cotta: literally "burnt earth"—a light, inexpensive clay material that holds brilliant colors.

Tracery: ornamental work of interlacing lines.

Travertine: a light-colored, porous marble.

Trompe l'oeil: a two-dimensional design that creates the illusion of a third dimension.

Turret: a small tower projecting from a building.

Verdigris: a greenish coating that forms on weathered brass, bronze, and copper.

INDEX

NOTES

_____

_____

_____

_____

_____

_____

_____

_____

_____

_____

_____

_____

_____

_____

_____

_____

_____

_____

NOTES

THE CELENASE
BUILDING

THE McGRAW·HILL
BUILDING

THE EXON BUILDING

NOTES

Student of life = make it
a loving experience —
you know what that
means.

ALSO AVAILABLE FROM CITY & COMPANY

Title	Price
The Big Cup: A Guide to NY's Coffee Culture	$12.95
City Baby: A Resource Guide for NYC Parents	$15.95
Beauty: The Little Black Book for NY's Glamour Girls	$12.95
Cool Parents Guide To All of New York	$12.95
Good & Cheap Ethnic Eats in NYC, 2nd Ed.	$16.00
Good & Cheap Vegetarian Dining	$9.95
How To Find an Apartment in New York	$12.95
How To Make NY a Better Place To Live	$9.95
How To Meet a Mensch in NY, 2nd Ed.	$12.95
Ken Druse's New York City Gardener	$15.00
Marden's Guide to Manhattan Booksellers, 2nd Ed.	$16.00
New York Book of Music	$15.00
New York Book of Dance	$14.00
New York Book of Tea, 2nd Ed. (cloth)	$16.00
New York Cat Owner's Guide	$9.95
New York Dog Owner's Guide	$9.95
New York Chocolate Lover's Guide (cloth)	$16.00
New York's 50 Hottest Nightspots, 2nd Ed.	$10.95
New York's 50 Best Places to Find Peace & Quiet	$10.95
New York's 50 Best Secret Architectural Treasures	$9.95
New York's 50 Best Things to Do at the Holidays	$12.00
New York's 50 Best Wonderful Little Hotels	$12.00
New York's 50 Best Places to Take Children	$12.00
Psychic New York	$13.00
Shop NY: Downtownstyle	$15.95
Shop NY: Jewelry	$15.95
A Year in New York (cloth)	$20.00

You can find all these books at your local bookstore, or write to:

CITY & COMPANY
22 West 23rd Street
New York, New York 10010
212.366.1988

ABOUT THE AUTHOR

Eric Nash is a researcher for *The New York Times Magazine*. He lives in one of the earliest tall apartment buildings in New York, the landmarked Beaux-Arts Apartments, designed by Raymond Hood in 1930. His other books include *New York's 50 Best Secret Architectural Treasures*.

ABOUT THE ARTIST

Robert Miles Parker came to New York fifteen years ago, as to a mecca. He founded San Diego's preservation society, Save Our Heritage Organization (SOHO), as an expression of his love of architecture. He has published three books of drawings: images of American architecture, of Los Angeles, and of the Upper West Side.